CRISTINA
AND
HER DOUBLE

ALSO BY HERTA MÜLLER

The Passport
Traveling on One Leg
Nadirs
The Land of Green Plums
The Appointment
The Hunger Angel

CRISTINA
AND
HER DOUBLE

Selected Essays

H ERTA M ÜLLER

Translated from the German by Geoffrey Mulligan

Portobello

*The translator would like to thank the distinguished poet Philip Schultz
for his invaluable work on the poems.*

Published by Portobello Books 2013

Portobello Books
12 Addison Avenue
London
W11 4QR

The translation of this work was supported by a grant from the Goethe-Institut which is funded by the German Ministry of Foreign Affairs.

A CIP catalogue record for this book is available from the British Library

9 8 7 6 5 4 3 2 1

ISBN 978 1 84627 475 6

www.portobellobooks.com

Typeset in Garamond by M Rules

Printed and bound by CPI Group (UK) Ltd, Croydon, CR0 4YY

CONTENTS

Always the Same Snow
and Always the Same Uncle

Seen from behind, the women's hairdos were sitting cats. Why do I have to say sitting cats to describe hair?

Everything always became something else. At first unobtrusively something else, if you just happened to look at it. But then demonstrably something else when you had to find the right words to describe it. If you want to be precise in your description, you have to find something completely different within the sentence to allow you to be precise.

Every woman in the village had a long, thick plait. The plait was folded back on itself and directed vertically upwards, and a rounded horn comb kept it standing proud above the middle of the head. The teeth of the horn comb vanished into the hair, and only the corners of its curved edge peeked out like small, pointed ears. With those ears and the thick plait, the back of the women's heads looked like a cat sitting bolt upright.

These vagabond qualities that turned one object into another were unpredictable. They distorted one's perception in the blink of an eye, made of it what they wished. Every thin branch swimming in the water resembled a water snake. Because of my constant fear of snakes I have been afraid of water. Not out of fear of drowning, but out of fear of snake wood, I never learned to swim for fear of scrawny, swimming branches. The imagined snakes had a more powerful effect than real ones could have, they were in my thoughts whenever I saw the river.

And whenever funerals approached the cemetery the bell was sounded. One long tug on the rope followed by the small bell with its rapid, urgent ringing – for me that was the cemetery snake that lured people towards death with its saccharine tongue, and the dead towards the caress of the grave. And those caresses soothed the dead, you could sense it from the breath of wind in the cemetery. What soothed the dead revolted me. The more it revolted me, the more I had to think about it. For there was always a breeze, always some cool or warm and dry wind. I was distressed by it. But instead of hurrying, only my breath came in a rush, and I carried the water slowly, watered the flowers slowly, lingered. Those imagined objects in my head with their vagabond qualities may have been an addiction. I was constantly looking for them, so they came looking for me. They ran after me like a mob, as if my fear could feed them. But they probably fed me, gave an image to my fear. And images, above all threatening ones, don't have to console, and therefore they don't have to disappoint, and therefore they never shatter. You can conjure up the same image again and again in your head. Thoroughly familiar, it becomes a support. The repetition made it new every time, and took care of me.

When my best friend came to say goodbye the day before I emigrated, as we embraced thinking we would never see each other again, because I would not be allowed back into the country and she would never be allowed out – as my friend was saying goodbye, we couldn't tear ourselves apart. She went to the door three times and each time she came back. Only after the third time did she leave, walking in a steady rhythm the length of the road. It was a straight road, so I could see her bright jacket getting smaller and smaller, and strangely enough becoming more garish as she went into the distance. I don't know, did the winter sun shine, it was February, did my eyes shine with tears, or did the material of her jacket gleam – one thing I do know, my eyes followed my friend and, as she walked away, her back shimmered like a silver spoon. So I was able to sum up our separation intuitively in two words. I called it silver spoon. And that was the simplest, most precise way to describe the whole event.

I don't trust language. At best I know from my own experience that, to be precise, it must always take something that doesn't belong to it. I have no idea why verbal images are so light-fingered, why the most valid comparison steals qualities it's not entitled to. The surprise comes about only through invention, and time and again it proves true that one gets close to the truth only with the invented surprise in the sentence. Only when one perception steals from another, one object seizes and uses the substance of another – only when that which is impossible in real life has become plausible in the sentence can the sentence hold its own before reality.

My mother believed that in our family fate always intervened during winter. When she emigrated with me from Rumania it was winter, February. Twenty years ago.

A couple of days before departure, one was allowed to send seventy kilos of luggage per person in advance from the customs post near the border. The luggage had to be packed in a large wooden crate with prescribed measurements. The village carpenter built it out of pale acacia wood.

I had completely forgotten this emigration crate. I hadn't given it a thought since 1987, since I got to Berlin. But then there came a time when I had to think about it for days on end, for it played an important role in world events. Our emigration crate made history, it was at the centre of world events, it had become a celebrity, was on television for days on end. What with one thing and another, when objects become independent, when in your head they slide for no reason whatsoever into other things, ever more into other things, the better your head knows that they have absolutely nothing to do with these other things: so I kept seeing our emigration crate on television because the Pope had died. His coffin looked just like the emigration crate. Then the whole emigration resurfaced.

At four in the morning my mother and I left on a lorry with the emigration crate. The journey to the customs post was five or six hours. We sat on the floor of the trailer and sheltered behind the crate. The night was ice cold, the moon was rocking up and down, your eyeballs felt too bulky, like frozen fruit in your forehead. Blinking was painful, as if a dusting of frost were in your eyes. At first the rocking of the moon was mild and gently curved, then it got colder, it began to sting, had been sharpened to a point. The night was not dark, but transparent, the snow seemed like a reflection of daylight. It was too cold to talk on this journey. You don't want to keep opening your mouth if your gums are freezing. I wasn't about to breathe a word. And then I had to speak, because my mother, perhaps intending only to mutter to herself, said out loud:

'It's always the same snow.'

She was referring to January 1945 and her deportation to the Soviet Union for forced labour. There were sixteen-year-olds on the Russians' lists. Many people hid. My mother spent four days in a hole in the ground in the neighbour's garden, behind the barn. Then the snow came. They couldn't bring her food in secret any more, every step between house, barn and hole in the ground became visible. Throughout the village, the way to every hiding place could be seen in all that snow. Footsteps could be read in the garden. People were denounced by the snow. Not just my mother, many people had to abandon their hiding places voluntarily, forced out voluntarily by the snow. And that meant five years in the work camp. My mother never forgave the snow.

Later, my grandmother said to me, 'You can't imitate freshly fallen snow, you can't rearrange snow so it looks undisturbed. You can rearrange earth,' she said, 'sand, even grass, if you take the trouble, water rearranges itself because it swallows everything including itself and closes over once it has swallowed. And air,' she said, 'is always arranged, because you can't even see it.'

Hence every substance other than snow would have remained silent. And to this day my mother believes the thick snow was mainly responsible for her being carted off. She felt that the snow fell on the village as if it knew where it was, as if it were at home here. But then it behaved like a stranger, straight away at the service of the Russians. Snow is a white betrayal. That is exactly what my mother meant by her sentence: It's always the same snow.

My mother never said the word BETRAYAL, she didn't need to. The word BETRAYAL was there because she didn't say it. And the word BETRAYAL even grew over the years the more she told her story without using the word BETRAYAL, in repeated sentences always with the same formulations that had no need of the word BETRAYAL. Much later, when I had long known the stories of being carted off, it occurred to me that by dint of systematic avoidance the word BETRAYAL had become monstrous in the telling, in fact so fundamental that, had you wished, you could have summed up the

6

entire story with the words SNOW BETRAYAL. The experience was so powerful that in the years to come perfectly common words were sufficient to tell the story, no abstractions, no exaggerations.

SNOW BETRAYAL is my phrase, and it's like SILVER SPOON. For long, complicated stories, a simple word contains so much that's unspoken because it avoids all details. Countless possibilities stretch out in the listener's imagination because such words curtail the course of the action to a single point. A phrase such as SNOW BETRAYAL allows many comparisons, because none has been made. A phrase like that leaps out of the sentence, as if made of a different material. I call this material: the trick with language. I am always afraid of this trick with language, and yet it's addictive. Afraid because, as I am engaged in the sleight of hand, I feel that if the trick succeeds, something beyond the words will become true. Because I am taken up for so long with succeeding, it is as if I wanted to prevent it. And because I know the gap between success and failure swings like a skipping rope, I know that in this instance it is the temples and not the feet that are skipping. Invented by means of the trick, and therefore entirely artificially, a phrase like SNOW BETRAYAL resonates. The material it is made of changes and becomes no different from a natural physical sensation.

I was responsible for the first betrayal I can remember: the betrayal with the calf. I had two calves in my head, and I measured one calf against the other, if not there would have been no betrayal. One calf was carried into the room, the other calf's foot was broken.

One calf was carried into the room shortly after it was born and placed on the sofa in front of my grandfather's bed. My grandfather had lain paralysed in this bed for years. And for fully half an hour he looked at the newborn calf in total silence with piercing, greedy eyes. I sat on the sofa at the foot of the bed and at the foot of the calf. And I watched my grandfather. Sympathy for him almost broke my heart, just as I was repulsed by his gaze. It was a thieving gaze, aimed directly at the calf, it stretched tight like a glass string in the air between bed and calf. It was a look in which the pupils shone like freshly soldered metal droplets. An obscene, despairing admiration that consumed the calf with the eyes. My grandfather could only see the new calf, he couldn't see me – thank God. For I could feel how all-consuming that gaze was, how shameless. What hunger in the eyes, I thought. Then HUNGER IN THE EYES was another phrase that kept coming into my head.

That was one calf. The other calf had its foot broken with an axe just after it was born, so that we could slaughter it. Killing calves was forbidden. They had to be handed over to the state after a couple of weeks, once they had reached the right weight. Only in the case of an accident did the vet allow enforced slaughter, and then one was allowed to keep and eat the meat. When my father explained the accident with the calf to the vet, how the cow had placed its heavy foot on the calf, I shouted, 'You're lying, you did it yourself with the axe!'

I was seven years old, I knew from my parents that one should never lie. But I also knew that the state is bad, and that it locked people up in prison because they told the truth. I knew too that the vet was a stranger in the village, against us and for the state. I almost caused my father to go to prison because he instinctively trusted me to distinguish between the lies that were not allowed at home and the white lies that were permitted because so much was forbidden. Once the vet had gone, after a hefty bribe, I understood, without knowing the word, what I had done, what betrayal is. I felt scorched. I felt sick from head to toe.

For years we had faithfully handed over every calf to the state. Now we wanted to eat veal. That's what it was about. But it was also about several principles, which got confused. Lies, truth and dignity. It was permissible to lie to the state whenever possible, because it was the only way to get your due, this I knew. My father's lie was effective, it was flexible, and necessary too. So what was it that caused me to betray my father in front of this vet? I was thinking of the other calf in my paternal grandparents' house, the one the self-same father carried from the stall into the room in his arms and placed on the velvet sofa. The calf on the sofa was not beautiful, because a calf has no place on a sofa. It was ugly, the way it just lay there, even if it could do nothing about the fact that it was a calf on a velvet sofa, that it was being so spoiled. But the calf whose foot had been broken with the axe was beautiful. Not out of pity, because we wanted to slaughter it. If you want to eat meat, you have to slaughter – no, the calf was beautiful precisely because we couldn't slaughter it but were obliged to put it on show and torment it. To my peasant eyes, that turned it into an impressive creature. Countless times every day I watched without the slightest problem as chickens, hares or goats were slaughtered. I knew how young cats were drowned, dogs slain, rats poisoned. But an unfamiliar feeling came over me because of the broken foot, I was taken by the natural beauty of the calf, its almost notoriously mawkish innocence, a kind of pain on witnessing the abuse. My father could have ended up in prison. Prison – the word struck me like a knife, in the emptiness of my betrayal my heart pounded up to my brow.

That was a different betrayal to SNOW BETRAYAL.

Perhaps I was reminded of the betrayal with the calf, with the two calves, because this night journey by lorry across the plain and the empty fields was as translucent as thin milk. Sitting in the slipstream of the emigration crate my mother had spoken only of SNOW BETRAYAL.

Then she was travelling to the camp in a sealed cattle wagon, and now she was travelling with me in a lorry to the customs point. Then she was guarded by soldiers with guns, now only the moon was watching. Then she was locked in, now she was emigrating. Then she was seventeen, now she was over sixty.

It was tough travelling on a lorry by moonlight through the February snow with sixty years and seventy kilos and an emigration crate, but it was nothing compared to 1945. After many years of harassment I wanted out of this country. Even if my nerves were

10

shot, even if I had to do it to escape the Ceauşescu regime and its secret service, and so as not to lose my mind, STILL it was something I wanted to do, not had to do. I wanted to get out, and she wanted to because I wanted to. I had to say that to her on the lorry, even if my gums froze as I was talking. 'Stop comparing, it's not the snow's fault,' I had to say to my mother, 'the snow didn't force us out of our hiding place.'

At that time I was not far from losing my mind. I was so exhausted my nerves were playing tricks on me, the fear I felt came through every pore and on to every object I tinkered with. They then tinkered with me. If you look just a little over the edge, manoeuvre just a little in that tiny space in your head between the abstruse and the normal, and if you watch yourself doing it, you have reached the farthest point of normality. Not much more can be added. One must keep an eye on oneself, try to separate thinking and feeling. One wants to absorb everything into the head as usual, but not into the heart. Inside yourself two versions stalk: one enlarged but totally strange, the other familiar but unrecognisably tiny and blurred. You feel yourself becoming increasingly unrecognisable, indistinct. This is a dangerous state to be in, however closely you pay attention you don't know when it will topple over. Only that it will topple over if this shitty life doesn't change.

It wasn't just that there was no hiding place in the snow, as I said to my mother, there was none in my head: it was clear to me I had to get away. I was at the end of my tether, for several months I had confused laughing and crying. I knew when not to cry, when not to laugh, but it was of no use. I knew what was right, and I did it all wrong. I was no longer able to keep to what I already knew. I laughed and I cried.

It was in this state that I arrived at the Langwasser transit hostel in Nuremberg. It was a tall tower block opposite the site of Hitler's rallies. The block contained little boxes for sleeping in, corridors with no windows, neon light only, countless offices. On day one there was an interrogation by the German Counter-Intelligence Service. Then again on the second day, repeatedly, with breaks, and on the third, and on the fourth. I understood: the Securitate weren't here with me in Nuremberg, only the German Counter-Intelligence Service. I was now where he was, but where was I, how the hell did I get here. Their interrogators were known as inspectors. The signs on the doors read Inspection Office A and Inspection Office B. Inspector A wanted to know if in fact I had 'an assignment'. The word 'spy' didn't come up, but they asked, 'Did you have anything to do with the secret service there?' 'It did with me, there is a difference,' I said. 'I'll be the judge of that, it's what I'm paid for,' he said. It was disgraceful. Inspector B then asked, 'Did you want to overthrow the regime? You can admit it now. It's yesterday's snow.'

Then it happened. I couldn't stand it that some inspector was dismissing my life with a saying. I leapt up from the chair and said, far too loudly, 'It's always the same snow.'

I have never liked the saying 'yesterday's snow', because it has no curiosity about what happened in the past. Now I knew clearly what it was I couldn't abide about the saying, the snows of yesteryear. I couldn't stand the meanness of it, the contempt. This expression must be very insecure to puff itself up like that, to appear so arrogant. We can gather from the expression that this snow was presumably important in the past, otherwise we wouldn't be talking about it, wouldn't be trying to rid ourselves of it today. What went through my head next I didn't say to the inspector.

In Rumanian there are two words for snow. One is the poetic word, *nea*. In Rumanian *nea* also means a man whom we know too well to address formally but not well enough to address familiarly. One might use the word UNCLE. Sometimes words determine their own uses. I had to defend myself against the inspector and against the suggestion in Rumanian that said to me, it's always the same snow and always the same uncle.

And something else happened when, newly arrived from the dictatorship to a Nuremberg transit hostel, I was being interrogated by a German Secret Service man. I've just been rescued, I thought, and I'm sitting here in the West like the calf on the sofa. Only when I saw the HUNGER IN THE EYES of the official did I understand not it was that only the tormented calf with the broken foot that had been abused, but also, every bit as much – only more insidiously – the spoiled calf on the sofa.

Every winter the white seamstress came to our house. She stayed for two weeks, ate and slept with us. We called her white because she only sewed white things: shirts and undershirts and nightshirts and brassieres and suspenders and bedclothes. I spent a lot of time near the sewing machine and watched the flow of the stitches, how they formed a seam. On her last evening in our house I said to her at dinner, 'Sew something for me to play with.'

She said, 'What should I sew for you?'

I said, 'Sew a piece of bread for me.'

She said, 'Then you'll have to eat everything you've played with.'

Eat everything you've played with. You could also describe writing that way. Who knows: what I write I must eat, what I don't write – eats me. The fact that I eat it doesn't make it disappear. And the fact that it eats me doesn't make me disappear. The same thing happens when words turn into something else as you write, to be precise, when objects proclaim their independence and verbal images steal what is not theirs. Especially when writing, when words become something different, to be precise, what is taking place is perhaps always the same snow and always the same uncle.

In Every Language There are Other Eyes

In the language of the village – so it seemed to me as a child – the words of all those around me lay directly on the things they denoted. Things were called just as they were, and they were just as they were called. An agreement concluded for all time. For most people there were no gaps that allowed them to glimpse between the word and the object and stare into nothingness, as if sliding out of one's skin into the void. Everyday actions were instinctive, the silent repetition of work, the head did not go along with the actions, nor did it follow its own distinctive paths. The head was there to carry the eyes and ears that were necessary for work. The expression: 'He's got his head on his shoulders so it doesn't rain into his neck' could be used to describe the daily life of everyone. Or perhaps not? When it was winter and there was no work to be done outside, when my father was falling-down drunk for days on end, why did my grandmother tell my mother, 'If you think you can't take it any longer, tidy up the cupboard'? Silence the head by moving the laundry around. The mother was to fold and stack, or hang up next to each other her blouses and his shirts, her stockings and his socks, her skirts and his trousers. Freshly laundered and laid out together, their clothes were supposed to prevent him from drinking his way out of this marriage.

Words only accompanied work when several people were engaged in a task and one was dependent on the actions of another. But even then that wasn't always the case. The heaviest work, such as carrying sacks, digging, hoeing, scything, was a school of silence. The body was under too much strain for it to waste energy on speech. Twenty or thirty people could remain silent for hours on end. Sometimes I thought, as I watched, that I was learning what happens when people forget how to speak. Once they cease toiling they will have forgotten every single word.

One's actions don't have to be replicated in words. Words hold up actions, they stand squarely in the way of the body – this I knew. But the absence of any correspondence between the hands on the outside and the head on the inside, the knowledge that you are now thinking something you are not entitled to and that no one believes you capable of, that was a different matter. That came only when fear came. I was no more fearful than other people. Like them I must have had many unfounded reasons to be afraid – reasons dreamed up and assembled in my head. But this dreamed-up fear is not merely imaginary, it is entirely valid when you have to grapple with it, for it is just as real as the fear that comes from outside. Precisely because it is assembled in the head one could call it headless fear. Headless because there is no precise cause and no remedy. Cioran said it was in our moments of groundless fear that we came closest to existence. The question: *what is my life worth?* provokes a sudden search for meaning, a nervous fever, a chill through the soul. This question set about dominating the everyday, gleamed out of moments of 'normality'. I didn't suffer the pangs of hunger, nor did I go barefoot, and in the evening I lay down to sleep in crisply ironed sheets in a newly made bed. Before the light was turned off the song: 'Now I lay me down to sleep,/ I pray the Lord my soul to keep' was sung to me. Then the tiled stove by the bed became a water tower, the one on the edge of town with the Virginia creeper. At that time I didn't know Helga M. Novak's lovely poem: 'The Virginia creeper round the water tower changes colour, it fades like the lower lips of the soldiers'. The prayer, which was meant to calm me and send me straight to sleep, had the opposite effect, it started my mind churning. That's why to this day I've never understood how faith can quell the fears of man, how it can give to others stability and lend itself to a calming of thoughts in the head. For every prayer became a paradigm, no matter how often it was rolled out. It demanded an appraisal of my own condition. The feet belong on the floor, higher up are the stomach, the ribs, the head. At the top comes the hair. And how does one lift one's heart through the hair,

17

then through a thick ceiling and up to God. Why does a grand-mother sing these words to me when she herself can't do what they ask.

In our dialect Virginia creeper is known as ink grapes because the dark berries colour the hands with spots that eat into the skin for days. The water tower beside the bed, its inky grapes the deep black of sleep. I knew that falling asleep meant drowning in ink. But I also knew, those who can't sleep have an uneasy conscience, an unwhole-some burden in their head. That's what I had, but I didn't know why. There was ink too in the village night outside. The tower had the area under its control, it tugged away earth and sky, leaving the villagers where they stood in a tiny fixed spot in the ink. From all sides came the croaking of frogs, the singing of crickets, pointing the way beneath the earth. And closing off the village into the echo of a crate, so no one could get away. Like all children, I was brought along to see the dead. They were laid out in their houses in the best room. We went to visit them one last time, before they were taken to the cemetery. The coffins were open, the feet pointed towards the door, the soles of the shoes upturned. We entered, walked round the coffin once, starting with the feet, and looked at the dead. The frogs and crickets were their staff. At night they said something transparent to the living to scramble their minds. To understand what they were saying I held my breath for as long as I could. In a panic, I gasped for air. I wanted to understand but not lose my head with no way back. Once you have understood the transparent,

I thought, you would be struck down and removed from this earth. The feeling that I was at the mercy of the local fodder in this village crate overcame me in the same manner on days of glaring heat in the river valley, where I had to mind the cattle. I had no watch, my watch was the railway line into town. There were four trains a day through the valley, and only after the fourth one had passed could I make my way home. Then it was eight o'clock in the evening. Then the sky too began to munch on grass and gathered up the valley. I hurried to get away before that happened. During those long days in a vast, bright green valley I asked myself countless times, *what is my life worth.* I pinched red marks in my skin to find out what sort of material these arms and legs were made of, and when God might want to reclaim that material. I ate leaves and flowers so my tongue was kin to them. I wanted us to resemble each other, for they knew how to live and I didn't. I called them by their names. The name 'milk thistle' was meant to be the prickly plant with milk in its stalk. But the name didn't suit the plant, which didn't answer to it. I tried out invented names: 'thorny rib', 'needle neck', where the words 'milk' and 'thistle' didn't appear. The trickery of all those false names before the right plant opened up the gap into the void. The humiliation of talking aloud to myself and not to the plant. The windows of the four passing trains were open, passengers standing in their short sleeves, and I waved. I approached as close as I could to the tracks, to catch a glimpse of the faces. The train was full of decent townsfolk, some of the women gleamed with jewellery and red nail varnish. When the train had passed my fluttering dress clung to me once more, my head was befuddled by the sudden stillness of the air, my eyes in pain, a merry-go-round crash landing. It was as if the eyeballs protruded too much and, cooled by suction, were too big for their sockets. I was breathless, the skin on my arms and legs filthy and scratched, my fingernails green and brown. After each train passed I felt abandoned, filled with self-loathing, and I took a closer look at myself. The valley sky turned a great filthy blue and the meadow a great filthy green, and I was caught between them, a tiny piece of filth that counted for nothing. The word 'lonely' does not exist in our dialect, only the word 'alone'. And that was '*alleenig*', and that sounds like '*wenig*', meaning 'not much' – and that's how it was.

That's how it was in the corn field too. Cobs with old man's hair, you could plait braids with it, broken yellow teeth, the grains of corn. One's own body rustled, was as small as the empty wind in the dust. Inside, the throat dry from thirst, above, an alien sun like a tray used by refined people to bring a guest a glass of water. To this day, tall corn fields make me sad, whenever I go past corn fields in a train or a car I close my eyes, overcome by the fear that corn fields circle the whole world.

I hated the stubborn field which consumed wild plants and animals to nourish cultivated plants and animals. Every ploughed field was an endless waxworks of the forms of death, a blooming funeral feast. Every landscape a rehearsed death. Flowers copied people's necks, noses, eyes, lips, tongues, fingers, navels, gave them no rest, borrowed their wax-yellow, chalk-white, blood-red or speckled blue body parts, coupled with green, they squandered what did not belong to them. The colours then rose through the dead man's skin at will. The living were foolish enough to demand the same, they bloomed on the dead because the flesh had surrendered. From my visits to the dead I was familiar with blue fingernails, yellow gristle in a greenish earlobe, where plants have sunk their teeth, impatient to get on with the work of decay, in the best rooms of the houses, not waiting for the grave. On the streets of this village, among its houses, fountains and trees, I thought: those are the fringes of the world, we should live on the carpet, it is made of asphalt and is only in the town. I had no desire to be captured by this blooming wax-works that squandered all colours, to place my body at the disposal of that greedy summer cauldron, camouflaged by blossoms. What I wanted was to move away from the fringes and on to the carpet, where the asphalt beneath your feet remains so solid that death can't come out of the ground and creep around your ankles. I wanted to go by train like a city lady with my nails painted red, to cross the asphalt with shoes dainty as lizards' heads, to hear the dry click-clack of my footsteps as I had on two visits to the doctor in town. Although I knew only peasants, I couldn't bear living within feeding range of plants, a reflection of leafy green on the skin. I was forever convinced that the fields were only feeding me so they could consume me. I didn't know how to give my life a context that made me aware that one is a permanent candidate for the waxworks of death.

It was a failure I found unconvincing, nor did anyone believe me capable of the thoughts running through my head. I had to rip open each moment so wide that no human action could fill it. I provoked the naked presence of transience, couldn't find an acceptable way of sticking to the everyday.

One is exposed when one leaves one's own skin and slips into the void. I wanted to get close to my surroundings and I became withdrawn from them, was so shattered by them that I could no longer piece myself together. Today it seems to me incestuous. I longed for a 'normal life' but cut myself off from it because I couldn't let anything rest. I badly needed inner calm but had no idea how to achieve it. I don't think there were any external signs. It didn't occur to me to talk about it. The disconnection in my head had to stay hidden. There were no words for it in our dialect apart from 'lazy' for the physical side and 'profound' for the psychological side. I had no words of my own for it. To this day I have none. It's not true that there are words for everything. Nor is it true that we always think in words. Even now many of my thoughts are not in words, I haven't found the words – not in village German, not in city German, not in Rumanian, not in East or West German. And not in any book. The inner regions don't correspond to language, they drag one to places where words are inadequate. It's often the decisive point about which nothing more can be said, and the impulse to talk about it is well taken because it runs right past. Only in the West have I come across the belief that talking can get the better of chaos. Talking doesn't bring order to life in the cornfield, or life on the asphalt. Only in the West have I come across the belief that what has no meaning cannot be endured.

What can talking do? When most of life is out of kilter, words too come crashing down. I have seen the words on my tongue come crashing down. I was sure that even the words I didn't have, had I had them, would have come crashing down, like the ones on my tongue. I never knew how many words one would need to cover up the disconnection in one's head. A disconnection that promptly distances itself from the words found for it. Which words are they, and how quickly would they have to come forward and change places with others to keep pace with thoughts. And what does 'keep pace with' mean? Thinking speaks with itself differently than words speak with thinking.

And yet the urge remains 'to be able to say it'. Had I not always had that urge, I wouldn't have gone so far as to try out names for the milk thistle, to call it by the right name. Without that urge I wouldn't have built a distance from those around me by trying to get close.

Objects were always important to me. Their look belonged to the image of the people who owned them. They will always belong to what and how a human being is, inseparably so. They are the part of the person furthest removed from the skin. And should they outlive their owners, the absent person wanders round in these objects left behind. After my father died, the hospital handed me his false teeth and his glasses. His smallest screwdrivers lay in a kitchen drawer among the cutlery. For as long as he lived my mother told him every few days that tools didn't belong there and he should clear them away. They stayed there for years after he died. My mother liked the sight of them. Even if their owner no longer sat at table, at least his tools should be among the cutlery. She stayed her hand, generous exceptions infiltrated her sense of order. I thought to myself, if he were to return to this table he could eat with his screwdrivers instead of a knife and fork. The stubborn apricot trees in the garden bloomed. Feelings are often transferred in a strange way. On to a handful of objects, which, for no particular reason, clarify memory. We follow crooked paths. It wasn't the false teeth or the glasses that portrayed the father's absence, but the screwdrivers and the apricot trees. I fixed my eyes so irrationally and so deep in to the trees that, if I looked for a long time, the still bare short branches became indistinguishable from the small screwdrivers. I was an adult then and yet things became jumbled up just as insidiously as when I was a child.

Berlin is not a place for growing apricots, too cold for that. I didn't miss apricot trees in Berlin. Then, without looking, I found one. It stands right by the tracks at an S-Bahn bridge. You can't get to it, it belongs to no one, except perhaps the state. It stands in a dip in the railway embankment. Its crown is as tall as the bridge railing but so far from it that you would have to lean perilously forward to pick apricots. I pass it every few days. For me the tree is a piece of village that got away, older than my time in Germany. As if the village and several trees within it had grown weary, as if they had run away from the garden, unnoticed. As if runaway trees behaved like runaway people: they leave the place of danger at just the right time, find a country that is halfway acceptable, though it's the wrong place to stay they cannot muster the resolve to leave. I pass the apricot tree on my way to the shop. There are two sides to the street, of course, and I could avoid it. The apricot tree makes it impossible simply to go into the shop. In choosing which side of the street to walk on, I am deciding whether to visit the tree or avoid it. The decision isn't earthshaking. I say to myself: let's see how the tree is today. Or: it can leave me in peace today. It's not the father who presses me to make these visits, not the village, not the country – certainly not homesickness. The tree is neither burden nor relief. It just stands there as an aftertaste of the time. What crackles in my head in its presence is half sugar, half sand. The German word *'Aprikosen'*, meaning apricots, is a flattering word. It sounds like *'liebkosen'*, to caress. After all those encounters with apricots I put together this collage:

Car park cats drag five or six paws
crackling on stairs like acacia pods
as we eat deformed apricots

and village cats sit on chairs noses twitching
rolling their glassy eyes
their whiskers breathing in their sleep
cold sweet apricots
offshoots of harm
to this day I greet the car park cats

I don't expect this text to give absolute clarity to the apricots. It can neither deny nor verify what troubles me with the apricots. It's rather texts by other authors that clarify something for me, not my own. And when sugar is half sand, it's not my own sentence but one by Alexandru Vona that comes to my rescue with its laconic poetic shock:

I thought about the riddle of accelerated processes of memory, which are so extensive and yet only take seconds, even when they portray the length of an entire day or even more in condensed form [. . .] The question is actually simple: Where does time go when we only need so little to experience again what remains to us.[1]

The places where I had to be wary of objects for reasons that are unclear come back again and again. The objects repeat themselves and seek me out. Alexandru Vona writes: 'There is an oppressive presence to objects whose purpose I don't know.'[2] Without purpose there is something sneaky about hats, unbeknownst to their owners, secrets slide between the hair and the silk lining. Most are unknown to me, but I can feel their presence when someone is bustling around in a hat. So to 'take off your hat' or to 'doff your hat' has little to do with showing respect and a great deal to do with 'offering your forehead', as the forehead is naked when the hat is removed. When the hat is removed its interior is revealed, the white silk lining. The hat can be any headgear with a white lining. Once when two secret service men came to the factory to torment me, they took off their fur hats simultaneously. The hats removed, the hair on both their heads stood up on end. The brain had raised the hair so it could quit the head – I could see it lurking in the silk lining. The two secret service men behaved despicably, arrogantly – but faced with the white silk lining they were pitifully helpless. That white gleam made me feel untouchable. I could withdraw from them, bright, impudent thoughts came into my head, and they had no idea what was protecting me. Little poems came to me, I recited them to myself, as if reading from the silk lining. And their necks seemed old, their cheeks worn – it was clear that when these two gentlemen were discussing my demise they would not be able to withstand their own. Whereas my poems were standing in the white silk, their two heads were laid to rest.

I like people with hats, because their brain is on display when they remove them. To this day I avert my eyes as the hat is removed. Don't look, or you'll see too much. I could never buy headgear with a white lining: my temples would throb, because I would instantly decide that the head can hide nothing from the hat's lining, keep no secrets.

I say all that, mention the apricot tree, the silk lining of the hats – but I cannot clarify in words what they cause in the head. Words are carved out for talking, maybe even precisely carved out. They are there for talking, perhaps writing too, but they fail to understand the screwdriver branches of the apricot trees and the brain hat. They are in no position to define what happens behind the forehead.

Reading books or even writing them brings no relief. If I have to explain why I find one book rigorous and another shallow, I can only point to the frequency of passages that bring forth a disconnection in the head, passages that draw my thoughts straight to places where no words can survive. The more frequently these passages occur in the text, the more rigorous the book; the sparser they are, the shallower the text. For me the criterion of a text's quality has always been: does it bring about a silent disconnection in the head. Every good sentence flows to a place in the head where what it triggers speaks in something other than words. And when I say books have changed me, that's why. Although the contrary is often stated in this respect, there is no difference between poetry and prose. Prose has to maintain the same density even though, because the distance is greater, it must be rendered differently. In an interview Bruno Ganz, who often performs poetry, says,

With poetry it's possible for one line to lay bare a vast space, beyond the sense conveyed by the words. In a strange way it crosses over itself with the next line, new spaces keep opening up. Not like a presentation of the evidence in linear prose. There it's a question of shifts, with verticals and strange movements. For me, poetry is to be found in a large space, enveloped with air. There is always more meaning, always more movement, than is expressed in words.[3]

Bruno Ganz has put his finger on what happens when a text carries you along. But it's true for all forms of literature, including prose. It can be austere. Hanna Krall wrote,

She was brought from the Gestapo in Vienna to Auschwitz. There she was in quarantine. After three months – she couldn't stay any longer, for her husband was waiting in Mauthausen – she went up to Dr Mengele on the ramp, said she was a nurse and asked if she could accompany the transport (...) Doctor Mengele, refined, polite, conducted a brief test on the ramp. 'How do you distinguish between bleeding from an artery and that from a vein?' he asked. She knew the answer, after all she had learned nursing at the typhus unit in the ghetto. 'How often does a person breathe in a minute?' Mengele asked. She didn't know, and she was frightened. 'How often does the heart beat in a minute?', he asked, like an understanding professor, who doesn't like to fail students in exams. 'That depends,' she answered, 'on whether the person is afraid, and how tall they are.' Doctor Mengele burst out laughing, and she noticed that he had a gap between his front teeth. Diastema, she remembered the term from her nursing course. That gap is called Diastema.[4]

Hanna Krall is documenting, retaining a demotic tone, the written sentences flow with calm precision, a bright stillness. The sentences speak and listen at the same time, and as I read they push me unbearably close to facts. Hanna Krall refrains from commenting, the amassing and arranging of the facts creates an unyielding directness, which begins to echo inside the head. The documented realities experienced by the author appear to tell their own story. Hannah Krall's brilliance is in not commenting and yet standing behind every sentence by discreet intervention. Stringent use of literary techniques with no fiction, merely through the sum of words, sequences, cuts. In Hanna Krall's books events are forced back into the trap of lived experience. Another example is Alexandru Vona. He works with fiction. But his fiction seems to have a documentary edge. Vona's sentences glisten because they are so spare. This is how he describes the feeling of being at home: '. . . in the evening when I enter the room in the dark and recognise the chair, because I know it must be there, even as I know that I wouldn't recognise it in a strange room that was equally immersed in darkness – in fact I don't see anything there.'[5] Or: 'The whole town was like the motionless form of the person in the next seat at a concert.'[6] Or: 'I pay more and more attention to my own facial expression than to that of the person I'm talking to, and yet I can barely say more about myself than what is mirrored in the eyes of the other person.'[7] In Vona's sentences the disconnection is provoked by the lapidary style, what is stated becomes estranged from itself, it expands into a paradigm, and I don't know how or by what means. From the sentence's appearance you don't believe it capable of triggering what happens in your head.

A text can also be metaphorical, visibly threaded through with images, as in the work of António Lobo Antunes, and so leads to disconnections in the head: 'Black caprices, raging melancholies, anxieties whose colour matched that of the clouds gathering over the ocean, pillows on pillows, replete with double chins, with taffeta.'[8]

The three authors quoted here achieve the same thing in my head in completely different ways: they bind me to their sentences and astound me to the extent that I stand outside myself again and must bring those sentences to bear on my own life. A good prose sentence is often praised for being lyrical. Perhaps because it stands on its own. But it resembles only a good sentence in poetry and not a flat one. It's simply a case of two good sentences resembling each other. The sentence: 'When the birds die, they drift belly up in the wind'[9] in Antunes's prose is self-evident. It only sounds like good poetry because it is also good prose.

There were enough traps in the objects and words to do with action, but not in the words to do with thinking. Then I ran away from the fringes of the world, walked on asphalt, on carpet. I was fifteen and came to town, encountered utterly different things and learned Rumanian. It was difficult at first, I spent a long time listening, was overwhelmed. I had lizard-skin shoes with their clip-clop, but I wasn't altogether myself. It was as if all that was left of me were the tips of my high-heeled shoes as I walked through town. I spoke as little as possible. Then after half a year it was suddenly almost all there, as if I didn't have to do anything, as if pavements, counters, trams and all the objects in the shops had learned this language for me.

When your surroundings only speak what you can't speak, you listen to the language along with the whole region. And if you stay long enough the time in the region learns the language for you. That was my experience, the head had no idea how it happened. I think we underestimate how much we listen to words. But listening is a preparation for speaking. One day the mouth began to speak of its own accord. Then Rumanian was like my own language. But in contrast to German, the words were astonished when I found myself involuntarily comparing them with my German words. Their trickiness was sensual, impudent and surprisingly beautiful.

In the village dialect we say: the wind GOES. In the High German that was spoken in school we say: the wind WAILS. And to my seven-year-old ears it sounded as if the wind had hurt itself. In

Rumanian we say: the wind HITS, *vîntul bate.* You could hear the sound of movement as you said 'hits', so the wind didn't hurt itself, but others. The wind ceasing is as different as the wind wailing. In German we say: the wind has lain down – flat and horizontal. In Rumanian we say: the wind has STOOD STILL, *vîntul a stat,* steep and vertical. The example of the wind is just one of the constant shifts that occur between languages. Almost every sentence is a different glance. Rumanian saw the world as differently as its words were different. It was also differently woven into the net of grammar.

Lily, *crin,* is masculine in Rumanian. A feminine lily undoubtedly looks different to a masculine lily. In German we are dealing with a lily lady, in Rumanian with a gentleman. If you know both ways of seeing they merge in your head. The feminine and the masculine view are broken up. In the lily a man and a woman are swaying in to each other. The object performs a little spectacle within itself, because it no longer knows itself. What does the lily become in two languages that are running side by side? A woman's nose in a man's face, a long, greenish palate or a white glove or collar. Does it smell of coming and going or of staying put. Through the meeting of two aspects of the lily, the closed lily of the two languages has become a mysterious never-ending event. An ambiguous lily remains restless in the head and is always saying something unexpected about itself and the world. You can see more in it than in the one-language lily.

Shifts occur between one language and another. The mother tongue faces up to the foreign tongue's different way of seeing. The mother tongue is acquired almost effortlessly, a dowry that simply comes to us. It's judged by a late arrival from elsewhere. From being entirely self-evident the words suddenly emit a random gleam. From now on the mother tongue is not the only place objects can reside, the word in the mother tongue is no longer the only measure of things. Of course our relationship to the mother tongue is unshakeable. We trust its heft, even if affected by the glance of the newly arrived language. We know that, however random, this instinctive measure is the safest and most vital we have. It's given gratis to our mouths, without having been consciously learned. The mother tongue is instantaneously and unconditionally there, like our own skin. And just as vulnerable when others despise, ignore or even ban it. In Rumania people like me who came from the dialect village with our meagre school High German to the national language of the city had a hard time. During my first two years in the city it was easier for me to find the right street in some unknown neighbourhood than to find the right word in the national language. Rumanian treated me like my pocket money. No sooner had something in the shop caught my eye than my money was not enough to pay for it. What I wanted to say had to be paid for with the corresponding words and there were many I didn't know, and the few I did know didn't occur to me in time. But today I know that this gradual progress, these faltering steps, that forced me to go below the level of my thoughts also gave me the time to marvel at the way the Rumanian language transformed objects. I know I'm fortunate this happened. How different is the view of the swallow in Rumanian, *rîndunica,* which also means a row of seats. How loaded that word is. The bird's name implies that the swallows sit tightly packed in black rows on the wire. Before I knew the Rumanian word I used to see it every summer. I was astonished that the swallow could be so beautifully named. Increasingly the Rumanian language had the more sensual, to my mind the more apt words than my mother tongue. I could no longer forego these shifts. Not when I spoke and not when I wrote. I have yet to write a sentence in Rumanian in my books. But Rumanian always accompanies me as I write, because it has grown into my own seeing.

No mother tongue suffers when its randomness becomes apparent in the seeing of other languages. On the contrary, holding one's own language up to the eyes of another leads to a solid relationship, a relaxed kind of love. I didn't love my mother tongue because it's better, but because it's the most familiar.

Sadly this instinctive faith in the mother tongue can be undermined. Following the destruction of the Jews under National Socialism, Paul Celan had to live with his mother tongue being the language of his mother's murderers. Even trapped down this cold alley, Celan was unable to shake it off. For this language was there in Celan's very first word. The speech had grown in his own head and had to stay there. Even when it smelled of the concentration camp's chimneys Celan had to endure this language as an intimate stammer, though he grew up among Yiddish, Rumanian and Russian, and French became his everyday language. It was quite different with Georges-Arthur Goldschmidt. Following the destruction of the Jews he rejected the German language and for decades wrote only in French. But he didn't forget German. And his last books, written in German, are so masterly that most books written in Germany seem feeble by comparison. You could also say that for a long time Goldschmidt was robbed of his mother tongue.

Many German writers are firmly of the view that, if it came to it, the mother tongue could replace everything else. Though it has never come to it, they say: LANGUAGE IS HOMELAND. Authors whose homeland is decidedly unthreatened, who are faced with nothing life-threatening at home, annoy me when they make this assertion. Any German who says: LANGUAGE IS HOMELAND is under some obligation to compare themselves to the people who coined the phrase. And it was coined by the emigrants who fled Hitler's murderers. When applied to them, LANGUAGE IS HOMELAND is reduced to naked self-assurance. It simply means: 'I still exist'. For emigrants who were without hope and far from home LANGUAGE IS HOMELAND was an assertion of their existence, formed in their own mouth. People whose homeland allows them to come and go as they please should not be flogging this phrase to death. The ground beneath their feet is safe. Coming from their mouths the phrase makes a mockery of the losses of those who fled. It suggests that emigrants could disregard the collapse of their existence, the loneliness, the shattering beyond repair of their self-image, because the mother tongue in their heads could act as a portable homeland and make it all good. It's not that you can take your language along with you, you have no choice. It's only when you're dead you don't carry it with you – but what's that got to do with homeland.

I don't like the word 'homeland'. In Rumania it was commandeered by two types of home owners. The first were the Swabian polka masters and moral guardians of the villages, the second were the functionaries and lackeys of the dictatorship. The village homeland as Germanic folklore and the state homeland as uncritical obedience and blind terror in the face of repression. Both concepts of homeland were provincial, xenophobic and arrogant. Everywhere they smelled of betrayal. Both needed enemies. Their judgements were malign, sweeping and immovable. Both were above ever reversing a false judgement. Both punished the entire family. After my first book was published the villagers spat in my face when they came across me in the street – I no longer dared to go into the village. And in the village the barber announced to my grandfather, a man of almost ninety who had been his client every week for decades, that from here on he would no longer shave him. And the farmers in the agricultural cooperative would no longer travel with my mother on the tractor or the horse and cart, they punished her in the endless corn fields, left her on her own, because she had this wicked daughter. She had been thrust into the same loneliness I knew as a child, though for different reasons. And she came to visit me in the city. In tears she tried not to reproach me when she said, 'Leave the village be, can't you write about something else. I have to live there, you don't.' And the gentlemen in the city hauled me off for an interrogation and ordered the village policeman to detain my mother for an entire day in his office. I didn't allow my family to influence my writing or my public pronouncements. I didn't tell them what I was doing, and they didn't ask. I wanted to exclude them from the risks I was running, whose meaning they didn't understand in any case. But in both village and state they were drawn by association into a responsibility that wasn't theirs. And I felt guilty and could change nothing, could not retract a single word, to them or to the state. Was this place home only because I knew the language of these two homeland factions? It was precisely because I knew them that we reached the stage where we could never speak the same language. The content of what we had to say was incompatible down to the smallest sentence.

There is a sentence of Jorge Semprún's that stays with me. It's in his book *The Autobiography of Federico Sanchez*, and it sums up the life in exile of the concentration camp survivor Semprún during the Franco dictatorship. 'It is not language that is homeland,' says Semprún, 'but that which is spoken.'[10] He knows that to belong to the homeland one needed to agree, even minimally, with the content of what is said. How could Spanish be a homeland to him in Franco's Spain. The content of the mother tongue went against his life. Rather than flirting with the notion of homeland at the most miserable point of existence, Semprún's insight HOMELAND IS THAT WHICH IS SPOKEN is contemplative. How many Iranians are thrown in prison to this day for one Persian sentence. And how many Chinese, Cubans, North Koreans and Iraqis cannot be at home for one second in their mother tongue. Could Sakharov find a homeland in Russian while under house arrest.

If life makes no sense any more, then words too collapse. For all dictatorships, whether of the right or the left, atheistic or theocratic, use language to their ends. In my first book about a childhood in a Banat Swabian village, the Rumanian publisher censored, along with much else, the word SUITCASE. It had become an inflammatory word because the emigration of the German minority was supposed to be a taboo subject. This seizure blindfolds the eyes of words and tries to erase the understanding of language inherent in words. The prescribed language becomes as malevolent as the degradation itself. We cannot speak of homeland here.

In Rumanian the roof of the mouth is called MOUTH HEAVEN, *cerul gurii*. This doesn't sound pompous in Rumanian. In Rumanian there are always new and unexpected ways of firing elaborate curses. In that respect German is positively buttoned up. I have often thought, if the roof of the mouth is a MOUTH HEAVEN, then there is a lot of room, and curses become infinite, angry poetic tirades of embitterment. A successful Rumanian curse is halfway up the palate, I used to say to Rumanian friends. That's why people in this dictatorship don't rebel. Cursing takes care of their anger.

Long after I could speak fluent and flawless Rumanian I listened in astonishment to the daredevil imagery of this language. The words came across as inconspicuous, but concealed an unerring political stance. Many a word contained stories that were related, without being spelled out. As in all poverty-stricken places, the country was full of cockroaches. And the cockroaches were called RUSSIANS, naked bulbs without a lampshade RUSSIAN CHANDE-LIERS, sunflower seeds RUSSIAN CHEWING GUM. Through sly, contemptuous word games ordinary people stood up daily against Big Brother. The connections remained hidden and were all the more derisive for that. When only smoked pig's trotters were avail-able in the shops instead of meat they were called gym shoes. It was impossible to prevent this type of extreme political commentary. Poverty made up the furnishings of daily life. If you mocked wretched objects you also mocked yourself. There were clear long-ings in this mockery, and that made it appealing. A dwarf worked as a messenger in the engineering plant. As the three divisions of the factory were spread around the town he delivered the files. When he knocked on the door you couldn't see him. His head didn't reach the window. In the factory he was known as MR-IS-NOT-THERE. Or gypsies who had put behind them the miseries of the clay huts and become furnace men or fitters in the factory were known contemptuously as SILK GYPSIES.

To admire the quick-witted, ever-present humour in the dictatorship is also to gloss over its failings. When humour derives from hopelessness, when its wit depends on desperation, the boundary between amusement and degradation becomes blurred. Humour requires punchlines, and only when they are merciless do they shine. There are verbal sparks. There were people who had a joke for everything, they were quick-witted, they had mastered variations and combinations, they were trained for jokes, pros at cracking jokes. But their training was so thorough that many of their jokes descended into the shabbiest racism. They turned misanthropy into a form of entertainment. Among colleagues in the factory who could tell jokes for hours on end I have sometimes noticed that this capacity did not only come about through verbal fireworks, but through looking down on everyone and everything around them. The arrogance contained in the punchlines became a habit. The jokers were suffering from an occupational hazard, they were deformed, missed the target without realising it. And so subversive jokes aimed at criminal state power went hand in hand with racist ones. With every practised joker I knew in the factory one could have produced a statistic of how many subversive jokes were made for each racist one.

The same is true of phrases or sayings with smooth rhymes whose singsong imprints itself instantly on the mind, and seems so complete that there is no need to puzzle over them, merely to repeat them. In the free market economy, advertising also uses the joke effect of sentences and images. When I came to Germany I was scared by a removal firm's advertisement that said: 'We'll give your furniture legs.' For me furniture with legs was a clue to the secret police's presence. I came home and the bedroom chair had moved to the kitchen in my absence. The picture on the wall had gone across the room and landed on the bed. At the moment an advertisement in Berlin bus stops features a woman's neck, with two fresh bullet holes. A drop of blood flows from the lower hole. It is an advertisement for the internet. In another advertisement a high-heeled shoe is pressing down on a man's hand. I can't do otherwise, I have to take these images seriously. They are an unnecessary and therefore a shabby violation, a senseless infringement. An impertinent game with torture and murder. What does the fact that a shoe is on a human hand have to do with its beauty. To my mind these methods degrade a firm's products. I couldn't buy the dainty shoe in the poster because of a crushed hand that goes with it. The crushed hand becomes inseparable from the shoe. It's even bigger than the shoe and it plagues me. The colours and the seams of the shoe have vanished, but the hand remains clear in my head. If I never see that poster again I could still show exactly how the man's hand lay as it was trodden on. I'm not surprised at what remains in the memory, it is what it is: in the face of brutality all beauty loses its wilfulness, turns into its opposite, becomes obscene. The same goes for beautiful people who abuse others, beautiful landscapes where misery resides, and the same goes too for lizard-skin shoes on the asphalt, even if the clip-clop of beautiful shoes turns my head. The advertisement for the shoe troubles me with the memory of real people tormented during the dictatorship, whom I saw shattered. For me, this dainty lizard-skin shoe in the poster is ready for anything. I could never own it, couldn't ever accept it as a present. I couldn't be sure this shoe wouldn't revert to its habit of treading on hands without my noticing.

Only someone who has no awareness that violence hurts and mutilates people can have dreamed up this advertisement. To load a shoe with this story is not to refine aesthetics but to infiltrate it with brutality. The size and stillness of these advertising posters places them daily before our eyes with a view to elevating it. The posters defame their product. Their stillness and size lodges in the skull. While waiting for the bus, pushing a pram, walking by with a shopping bag, the vital threshold beyond which something causes pain to another person is lowered daily. The recognition of brutality slides beneath what is acceptable. As these posters impose themselves before my eyes I would like to ask the maker of the shoe and the advertisement: where does this lead you, where will the lizard-skin shoe take you.

Every day I decide to ignore the posters, and still I look at them. In a cynical way, the advertising works well with me. But the consequences are the opposite. They don't count on customers like me, who would love to have the lizard-skin shoe were it not compromised by this advertising. I fear the people who made the poster are not stupid, but rather realistic: most customers aren't disturbed by the posters, aren't put off by them, on the contrary they are impelled to buy. They can happily do without the handful who take it all seriously.

I have often watched my father spitting on his shoes, rubbing the spit in with a cloth before he left the house. The spat-upon shoes sparkled. Spit was applied to mosquito bites, thorn pricks, burns, grazed elbows and knees. We used spit to rub streaks of dirt from stockings and the hems of coats, or dirt from the skin. As a child I thought: spit is good for everything. In summer it's cool on the skin, in winter it's warm. Then I learned about the drills of the SS and the Wehrmacht. Sparkling shoes were part of it. And when I saw my father spitting on his shoes I thought: he learned that from the Nazis. The little details show best that the SS soldier still remains within him. I knew from friends who had to serve in the army before their studies that in that run-down Rumanian army ruled a mania for shoe cleaning. At manoeuvres the soldiers had no bullets to fire, they were too expensive, but they had spit in their mouths. The less they were able to practise shooting, the more they practised shoe cleaning. No shoe polish in the country. A friend of mine, a viola player, had to clean the officers' shoes for three days, till his throat was dry from all the spitting and his hands were so blistered he couldn't practise his viola for the next few weeks.

Recently I read something else to do with soldiers and spit. Peter Nádas writes about the suppression of the Prague Spring, when the Hungarian army marched in to Czechoslovakia in 1968 along with the armed forces of the Warsaw Pact: 'On the journey to Prague, the windscreen wipers of the Hungarian military vehicles no longer worked because of the sheer volume of spit on the windscreens, and the Hungarian soldiers trembled and cried behind them ...' Spit used by civilians as a weapon against an army.

When a child bore a close resemblance to the father or mother, we said in the language of the village: the child is the spit and image of the father (or the child is the spit and image of the mother). The region I come from must have had a strangely uninhibited relationship with spit. Otherwise this rather insulting expression wouldn't have been seen as dispassionate or even friendly. But in the same region you could also say of a person: he's as bad as spit. And this short utterance was the nastiest insult you could hurl at someone. Spitting and talking are related. As Nádas shows, spitting begins when words are no longer enough to express contempt. Spitting at someone surpasses any curse. Spitting is a hard physical altercation.

In Rumanian, as in most Latin languages, the sounds are supple and one word quickly melds into another, there was no occasion that didn't have its rhyme, its adage, its saying. Falls and fractures were always accompanied by irreverent commentaries. As with the jokes, you had to listen twice and decide whether to adopt it, or never to let it pass your lips. 'Seen from afar a gypsy is a human being too,' was heard as often in spring as the phrase, 'From now on each day will be a crowfoot longer,' as the evenings grew lighter, or in the autumn, 'From now on each day will be a crowfoot shorter.' In every language the imaginativeness of sayings swings between a slap in the face and the velvet paw of words.

An acquaintance from southern Germany told me a story from the post-war Germany of his childhood. The firecrackers with long fuses that even small children throw into the night on New Year's Eve are called JEW'S FARTS. Whenever he heard the expression he always understood JUDO FARTS, he thought the name of the firecracker had something to do with the sport of JUDO. He believed this until he was seventeen, and through all those years, both at home and in the shop buying firecrackers, he asked for JUDO FARTS. In all that time neither his father and mother nor a single shop assistant corrected him. This acquaintance said that when he found out the real name, he felt ashamed of himself in retrospect for every New Year's firecracker that had exploded. His father was already dead by the time he understood the anti-Semitic name. His mother is still alive, he said, but to this day he couldn't bring himself to ask her how, having been in Auschwitz, she could still call firecrackers JEW'S FARTS without embarrassment. I wanted to know why he couldn't ask his mother. He shrugged.

Nowhere and at no time was or is language a non-political preserve, it cannot be separated from what one person does to another.

It always lives in the individual case. Every time we must listen to what its intentions are. Inseparable from action, it becomes legitimate or unacceptable, beautiful or ugly, you could also say: good or evil. In every language, in every way of speaking, there are other eyes.

Cristina and Her Double

or

What Does Not Appear in the Securitate Files

For me every journey to Rumania is also a journey into another time, a time when I never knew which part of my own life was down to chance and which was staged. That's why I've always demanded access to my Stasi files in all my public statements, something that was always refused for reasons that kept changing. Instead there were signs that yet again I was under observation.

Last spring I was invited to Bucharest by the NEC (New European College). On day one, as I was sitting in the hotel lobby with a journalist and a photographer, a muscular guard asked to see authorisation and grabbed the photographer's camera. 'No photos allowed here, including photos of people,' he ranted. The blue European flag stood upright at the reception desk – it was only a few days after the NATO conference in Bucharest. The journalist was cowed: 'Forgive us, it won't happen again.' The photographer was trying to rescue his camera. I asked the guard if the hotel lobby was a secret location and what the European flag was doing at the reception. He should shove it in a drawer, the EU and NATO are organisations that belong to a free world. And I said what he was doing here reminded me of the Ceauşescu times. Only then did he let go of the camera. But the surprises didn't stop there. On the second day I had a dinner engagement. As agreed on the phone, a friend came to collect me from the hotel at six o'clock. As he turned into the street leading to the hotel he noticed that he was being followed, and that the man stepped into the lobby after him, then leafed through the newspapers while my friend was asking reception to call my room and let me know he was waiting downstairs. The receptionist told him he would first have to fill in a visitor's form. He was shocked, such a document had never existed, not even under Ceauşescu.

My friend and I walked to the restaurant. On our way there he kept suggesting we take another street. I thought nothing of it. It wasn't till the next day, when I told Andrei Pleşu, the director of the NEC, the story about the guard, that my friend told him he had been required to fill in a visitor's form, and that a man had followed him to the hotel and then the two of us to the restaurant. Andrei Pleşu was horrified, he had always put his NEC guests up there. The next morning he sent his secretary to the hotel to cancel all the bookings. The hotel manager cooked up a story that it was the receptionist's first day at work, that she had made a mistake. But his secretary knew the woman, she had stood at the reception desk for years. The manager then said the owner of the hotel was a former Securitate man, who was unfortunately not willing to change his ways. He smiled and said the NEC could indeed cancel their bookings here, but it was no different in the other hotels of this category, it was just that people didn't know it.

I moved out and spent the remaining two days staying at an NEC office. I didn't notice any further harassment after that. Either the secret service withdrew because things were getting tricky, or they worked more professionally, which is to say invisibly.

They would have had to listen in to my hotel phone to know that they needed a tail at six o'clock. The TV in the hotel room showed CNN, BBC, RAI and UNO, and there was a bug on the phone. An EU flag at reception, and gumshoes following you around. That's democracy Rumanian style. It's widely known that Ceauşescu's secret service, the Securitate, was not dissolved but merely renamed the Rumanian Information Service (SRI). By their own account they absorbed forty per cent of the Securitate, that is, the younger, more agile personnel. The true percentage is probably greater. The remaining sixty per cent are either pensioners with pensions three times higher than everyone else, or the new movers in the market economy. In the early chaotic days of political transition they squirrelled away their 'bargains' – banks, factories, hotels, travel agencies, petrol stations and so forth. And those bargains swell daily into the ample fortunes of a trouble-free life. The bargain millionaires all know each other and help each other out on all levels. Their net stretches across the land from parliament through the economy, law, universities, even hospitals. It gives rise to ubiquitous corruption and will not be disrupted by anything in the near or distant future. In any case attempts to disrupt it are extremely rare. Where would they come from when full-time functionaries are well provided for and informers remain in their posts with impunity? In Rumania today a former spy can be almost anything he was previously, other than a diplomat.

Inspection of the Files in Rumanian

One of the best-known Rumanian authors, the grande dame of Rumanian poetry, said in an interview in Switzerland that she didn't want to look at her files, preferred rather to believe that everybody loved her. A woman of almost eighty, she'd lived through the gruesome Stalin years followed by the dismal Ceaușescu times. With such trivial statements she feigned naïvety. In truth she knows that betrayal was rampant, infiltrating relationships, sparing nobody's feelings. Love was meat and drink for betrayal – by allowing the greatest intimacy, it nurtures the greatest betrayal, poisons what is most intimate. This poet also pointed out that by wearing big summer hats she stood for the bourgeois lady against the socialist comrade. I knew her during the time of the big summer hats – they were hats, no more, no less. Her political opposition in hat form is new. Something not so new that I remember well: as editor of the magazine *People and Culture* the hat lady had misappropriated the poems of some authors for a socialist holiday edition of the magazine. As their poems had absolutely nothing to do with the holiday and their authors would never, ever have written poems celebrating such a holiday, the editor had taken existing poems without their knowledge, and replaced the original titles of the poems with fabricated titles celebrating the holiday. Thus she was able to fulfil her task as editor. That she was misappropriating poems and compromising authors did not prevent her from performing her duty. She suppressed her bad conscience to such a degree that the fear of losing her job as editor was greater than the shame in the eyes of the authors, whose position she knew. They were horrified at this fait accompli, but at the time there was no way of taking a public stance against this bogus party jubilation in any other journal in the entire country. The hat lady does not tell this story. Conversations about the dictatorship make her nervous. In interviews she says there were also happy moments during the dictatorship. Who could argue with that? Every human being has experienced those, but in spite of the dictatorship and not because of the dictatorship. In those private niches where harassment had not yet infiltrated – or even in opposition to the harassment there were erratic moments of fleeting and therefore wild, even passionate happiness. There was utterly personal, fleeting happiness in the gaps in state control. This happiness had to be as light-footed as betrayal, for it had to run away from betrayal or even outrun it. This form of happiness was often a light-fingered, limping happiness. We laughed to the point of exhaustion, and it resounded like the abyss. We cracked jokes about the secret service types and their harassment, crass, vulgar jokes. It was laughter at all costs, a close companion of fear. It was a well-rehearsed pantomime, a bitter necessity to make it possible for us to endure reality. Does a happiness such as this diminish the contempt for humanity that was every day evident during those times? If there was a bug in every room, as I have now learned from looking at my files, one's every private corner was being recorded by the state. Every time you caught your breath while laughing in a room in your own home was logged, without your knowledge, as a subversive action in the prosecution files. The hat lady has always disrupted discussion of the dictatorship. For twenty years now she has been coming up with, haven't we had enough on that subject. And she enjoys the support of far too many Rumanian intellectuals. Recently she said to me, I would never allow myself to say about Germany the things you say about Rumania. My answer was, you would have no reason to do so.

One is grateful when well-known Rumanian writers ignore discussion of the dictatorship and don't block or impede it by offering protection to the perpetrators. In Rumania the majority of intellectuals were as little troubled by the opening of the secret service files as by the shattered lives around them, and the same applies to the new arrangements of the party bigwigs and secret service men. If, like me, you spent years publicly demanding access to the files at every opportunity, you even began to get on your friends' nerves. Another reason why, instead of being handed over to the files authority (with the tongue-twisting acronym CNSAS) reluctantly established in 1999 under pressure from the EU, the files sat around for years in the keeping of the new-old secret service. They controlled access to the files at will. The authority had to forward requests to them, which were sometimes approved but mostly refused, even with the justification: work still in progress on file in question. The Rumanian Gauck Commission was a fig leaf from the start, and its workings are obscure to this day.

In 2004 I was in Bucharest and had gone to see them to reiterate my repeated request for access to the files. I was astonished: three young ladies were standing at the door dressed in sheer gloss tights, miniskirts and a deep décolleté, as if one were entering an Eros Centre. Between the ladies stood a soldier with a machine gun on his shoulder, as if one were entering a highly secret military barracks. I was informed the man in charge of the authority was not available, even though I had an appointment with him.

It seems my file could not be located. Yet this spring a group of researchers was gradually unearthing the files of Rumanian authors belonging to the 'Banat Action Group'. The Securitate had a specialised department for every minority. For the Germans it bore the name: 'German Nationalists and Fascists', the Hungarian section was called: 'Hungarian Irredentists', the Jewish: 'Jewish Nationalists'. Only Rumanian authors had the honour of being under surveillance by the 'Art and Culture' department.

Suddenly my file was discovered under the name CRISTINA. Three volumes, 914 pages. It was supposedly opened on 8 March 1983 – yet it also contains documents from years before. Reason for starting the file: 'Politically biased distortions of the realities in the country, especially in the village milieu' in my book *Nadirs*. The claim is substantiated by 'textual analysis' carried out by spies. I belong to: 'a circle of German-speaking writers known for their hostile works'.

The file is a concoction of the old Securitate in the name of the SRI. Over a ten-year period they had all the time they needed to 'work on it'. You couldn't call it manipulation, the file has had the heart ripped out of it. The most important things have been erased, along with anything that could be a liability for the functionaries themselves.

This purging is by no means unique. Andrei Pleşu, who was on the board of trustees when the CNSAS was founded, has long since left this committee, embittered and in protest. He had seen his own files once in the archive and knew that they were around 2,000 pages. When they were finally handed over to him they consisted of only seventy pages.

Besides giving access to the files, the CNSAS was also legally

obliged to elicit the actual names of the spies. All those who have so
far had access to their files tell the same story: the authorities sought
out one single name from the long list of spies, and revealed their
actual name. And this one person is either of minimal importance
in the file, or he is dead. The authority doesn't seem to want to track
down the decisive spies, the gross betrayals that went on all around
us. Is this a boycott? Is the authority somehow working against its
own interests? On whose orders?

After my studies I worked for three years as a translator in the
Tehnometal tractor factory. There is no mention of those three years
in my file. I translated instructions for the assembly and maintenance
of machines imported from the GDR, Austria and Switzerland. For
two years I sat in an office with four bookkeepers. They calculated
the wages of the workers, I pored over my fat technical dictionaries.
I had studied philology so I understood nothing about hydraulic or
non-hydraulic presses, threads or levers. When faced with a choice
between three, four or even seven terms, I used to go on to the shop
floor and ask the workers. Without knowing any German, they gave
me the correct Rumanian word – they knew their machines. In the
third year an 'Office of Protocol' was established. The director transferred me there to join two newly employed translators, one for
French, one for English. The French lady was the wife of a university
professor who was said to be a secret service man back when I was a
student. The English lady was the daughter-in-law of the second
most senior secret service man in the city. Only the two of them had

the key to the middle door of the filing cabinet. When foreign specialists came I had to leave the office. Then it seemed I was being lined up for this office after secret serviceman Stana made two attempts to recruit me. After my second refusal he hurled a vase of tulips against the wall. He walked through the pool of water and glass shards to the door. His farewell greeting: 'You'll be sorry. We'll drown you in the river.' I asked the director of the factory for a transfer back to my old office. I was to stay where I was, he said, stop worrying, and keep working on my translations, that's what I was there for. One morning I turned up for work and my dictionaries were on the floor in the corridor, by the office door. An engineer was at my desk. I was no longer allowed entry to the office. I couldn't go home or they would have been able to fire me without notice on account of unauthorised absence. I had no desk, no chair. After that I sat stubbornly for the whole eight hours with my dictionaries on a concrete step between the ground floor and the first floor and tried to translate, so nobody could say I wasn't working. Office workers streamed past me in silence. My friend Jenny, an engineer, knew what was going on. I told her everything that had happened each day on the way home. During the lunch break she came and sat down on the stair. We ate together, just as we did in my office. From the loudspeakers in the courtyard workers' choruses sang as ever about the happiness and progress of the people. As she ate, she was in tears for me. Not I. I had to tough it out. On the third day I installed myself at Jenny's desk. She made a corner free for me. On the fourth too. It was a large drafting office with drawing boards and around twenty desks. On the fifth morning she was waiting for me at the door: 'I can't let you come into the office any more. Just imagine, my colleagues say you're an informer.' 'How is that possible?' I asked. 'You know where we live,' she said. I picked up my dictionaries and sat on the stairs. This time I cried. When I came on to the shop floor to ask about a word, the workers whistled after me and shouted: 'Securitate stooge!' This was a witches' cauldron. How many informers might there have been in Jenny's office and on that shop floor? They were hard at work. These attacks were directed from above. The defamations were intended to force me to resign. My father died just as this turbulent time began. I was out of control, had to reassure myself of my place in the world. I began to write down my life up to this point – where I came from, the rigid three hundred-year-old village, the peasants with their silence, the father with his truck on the bumpy roads, his drunkenness and his Nazi songs with the 'comrades'. The mother, tough and bewildered, as if offended by life, forever in the endless corn fields. And I was in this factory with machines the size of a house, pools of oil everywhere, like mirrors that allowed you to slide vertically into the ground. The piecework at the production line, the mechanical hand gestures, the drained eyes, gazes like old zinc. That's where the short stories in *Nadirs* came from.

There is one word about the recruitment in my file, written by hand in the margin on the minutes of a wiretap transcription. Years later, at home, I was telling someone about the attempt to recruit me in the factory. In the margin, first lieutenant Padurariu had written: 'True.'

That I was now considered an informer because I had refused to become an informer was worse than the attempted recruitment and the death threat. I was being maligned by the very people I was sparing by refusing to inform on them. Jenny and a handful of colleagues knew the game they were playing. But all the rest, who only knew me by sight, didn't. How could I have explained to them what was going on, proved that it was the opposite of what it seemed. It was not humanly possible and the Securitate knew it, and that's precisely why they cooked it up. They also knew that this perfidy would destroy me more than all their blackmail. You can get used to death threats. They are part of the only way of life one has, because one can have no other. You defy fear, deep in your soul. But the slander robs you of your soul. You are completely surrounded. You almost suffocate from helplessness.

I can't recall how long I worked on that staircase, it seemed endless but was probably only a matter of weeks. Eventually I was fired.

During interrogations the same secret service that had engineered my dismissal now called me 'a parasitical element'. I was advised that the penalty for parasitical behaviour was prison or forced labour on building sites. The 'canal' was the big threat – Ceauşescu was having a canal built to link Bucharest with the Black Sea. It was a ludicrous construction, many soldiers and prisoners lost their lives there. When the canal was completed, it turned out it was of no use to shipping, it wasn't deep enough.

I had no money. Jenny found me some private tuition. I gave children German lessons or helped with their school work. But I went to each house two or three times at most. Then the secret service showed up and threatened the parents. When asking me not to come back, some said, 'You are harming our family. You see, we don't get involved in politics.' Others lied, said they could no longer afford private lessons because of a cut in wages. Soon I learned from the interrogations that I was allegedly living off prostitution and the black market, surely I must know that the penalty for it, as for parasitical behaviour, was prison. Names of clients and tricks were produced, names I had never heard. Added to this was spying for the German Intelligence Service, because I was friendly with a librarian at the Goethe Institute and an interpreter at the German embassy in Bucharest. Hour after hour of bogus accusations. But that wasn't all.

I was simply picked up from the street, no summons. While I was on my way to the hairdresser a policeman brought me through a narrow iron door into the basement of a student hostel. Three men in civilian clothes were seated at a table. The small, scrawny one was the boss. He asked for my identity card, 'We meet again, you whore,' he said. I had never met him. I was alleged to have had sex with eight Arab students and taken payment in stockings and cosmetics. 'I don't know a single Arab student,' I said. 'We'll find twenty Arab witnesses if we want to,' he replied. 'You'll see. It'll be a fine trial.' He kept tossing my identity card on the floor, and I had to bend down and pick it up. The thirtieth or fortieth time, as I had slowed down, he kicked me in the small of my back. Behind the door at the far end of the table I heard a woman's scream. Torture or rape, I thought, perhaps just a tape recording. I was forced to eat eight hard-boiled eggs and green onions with coarse salt. I forced the stuff down. Then the scrawny one opened the iron door, threw my identity card into the street and kicked me in the backside. I fell face forward in the grass next to a patch of scrub. I vomited without raising my head. In no hurry, I picked up my identity card and went back home. Being lifted from the street was more frightening than a summons. No one knew where you were. You could have vanished and never resurfaced or, as they had threatened back then, been hauled out of the river as a floater. The verdict: suicide.

No interrogation in the files, no summons, no lifting from the street.

What is recorded in the files on 30 November 1986: 'Every journey CRISTINA makes to Bucharest and elsewhere in the country must be reported promptly to the executive of the I/A [Internal Opposition] and III/A [Defence Against Espionage], to 'ensure permanent control'. I was not to travel anywhere in the country without being followed, so as to 'enforce the requisite methods of control in her relationships with West German diplomats and West German citizens'.

The tailing varied according to their intentions. Sometimes I was unaware of them, sometimes I noticed them, flew into a rage and became aggressive. When *Nadirs* was due to be published by the West Berlin based Rotbuch Verlag, to keep a low profile the editor and I had arranged to meet at Poiana Braşov in the Carpathian mountains. We travelled there separately, as if for winter sports. My husband, Richard Wagner, had driven back to Bucharest with the manuscript, I was to follow on the night train the next day without the manuscript. Two men greeted me in the concourse at Timisoara station and demanded to search my bag. I refused. They wanted to take me with them. 'I'm not coming along without a summons,' I said stubbornly. Perhaps it was too risky to cause a stir in the crowded concourse, for they didn't take me with them.

They confiscated my ticket and my identity card and, before leaving, ordered me not to move from the spot until they returned. I didn't move from the spot. Then the train arrived, and they hadn't come back. I went to the platform. This was the time of the great electricity initiatives, and the sleeper carriage at the end of the platform was in darkness. One was only permitted to board the train shortly before departure and the door was still locked. The two men reappeared, walking up and down, sometimes right beside me, then they jostled me three times, shoving me to the ground. Filthy and disoriented each time, I quickly got to my feet so I could stand there as if nothing had happened. The other passengers looked on as if nothing had happened. When the door of the sleeper carriage finally opened I shoved into the middle of the queue. The two men boarded as well. I walked into the compartment, got partly undressed and slipped my pyjamas over my clothes so people would notice if I was dragged out of there. When the train set off I went to the toilet and hid a letter for Amnesty International behind a pipe. The two men were standing in the corridor speaking with the train conductor. I had the lower bunk in the compartment, it was easier to grab me there, I thought. When the conductor came to my compartment he handed me the ticket and the identity card. I asked him where they came from and what the two men had wanted from him. 'What men?' he said. 'There are dozens here.'

I didn't get a moment's sleep the whole night. It was madness getting on board, I thought, they will throw me under the train somewhere out there in the empty snowfield. When the first grey light came my fear abated. They would surely have used the darkness for a staged suicide, I thought. Before the first passengers woke up, I went to the toilet and retrieved the letter. Then I got dressed, sat on the edge of the bed and waited for the train to enter Bucharest. I got off as if nothing had happened. No mention of this episode in the files either.

Being tailed had consequences for other people too. A friend caught the eye of the secret service for the first time at a reading I gave from *Nadirs* at the Bucharest Goethe Institute. After that his personal details were gathered, a file was opened and he was under surveillance. There is a record of it in his file, but not a word in mine.

When we were away from home the secret service came and went as they pleased. They would often leave deliberate signs: cigarette butts, pictures moved from the wall to the bed, the chairs moved around. Their most sinister stunt they dragged out over weeks. We had a fox skin on the floor. Gradually the fox's penis, paws and finally its head were cut off and laid out on the fox's stomach. It was psychological terror, seamless. While I was cleaning I first noticed the cut off penis lying there. I still thought it was down to chance. When weeks later a back foot was cut off I shuddered. Until the head was cut off, the first thing I did when I got home was to check on the fox skin. Anything could happen, the flat had lost all privacy. Every time I ate I thought the food might be poisoned. Not a word about these visits to my flat in the file.

In the summer of 1986, the writer Anna Jonas visited us in Timisoara. On 4 November 1985 she and other authors had written a letter – which is in my file – to the Rumanian Writers' Union, protesting that I was not allowed to attend the book fair or the Protestant church congress or to travel to my publishers. The 1986 visit is precisely documented in my file, and there is a telex of 18 August 1986 to the border agency, instructing them to search her luggage 'as thoroughly as possible' on her journey home and report on the results. The record of this visit is in my file, unlike the visit of the *Zeit* journalist, Rolf Michaelis. Following the publication of *Nadirs* he wanted to have a conversation with me. He announced his arrival by telegram, telling me he would meet me at home. But the telegram was intercepted by the secret service and my husband and I had gone to spend a few days in the country with his parents. For two days he rang the bell to the flat in vain. On the second day three men were watching him from behind the garbage chute and they gave him a savage beating. The toes of both his feet were broken. We lived on the fifth floor and the lift wasn't working because there was no electricity. Rolf Michaelis had to crawl on all fours through the darkness of the stairwell down to the street. The telegram from Michaelis is missing from the file, though a whole collection of confiscated letters from the West is there. According to the file the visit never happened. This absence shows yet again that the secret service systematically expunged its actions from the files and thereby ensured their senior figures could never be held to account through the files. Ensured that the Securitate post-Ceaușescu became an abstract monster where no one was responsible.

That's how I explain to myself other bizarre episodes that have no reference in my file:

On my first visit to Germany I lived at Ernst Wichner's in Berlin. He drove to visit his parents-in-law for a few days. The following day the doorbell rang. A technician announced that he was there to repair the telephone. It felt suspicious, so instinctively I did the right thing and sent him away. But I wasn't convinced I'd done the right thing. I picked up the phone and rang Ernst Wichner. He hadn't called up any tradesmen. About two hours later I left the house. The 'technician' was still sitting in his car.

On this first visit the people in the publishing house told me they had had two break-ins. One was at the editor's home and the other in the publishing house. Nothing was missing from the editor's home, the manuscripts had been jumbled up, but the publishers weren't suspicious. Even though the publishing house had also been broken into, they were naïve enough to think the burglar wanted to steal dental gold from the dentist below and had got the wrong floor. Maybe they weren't so naïve after all, just wanted to spare me knowing what was likely to happen to me every day after my return to Rumania. In my file there is a photo of me with the publishing house staff. Maybe that's a souvenir of the burglary.

When I was living in Berlin I was summoned to the Office for the Protection of the Constitution. I was shown a photograph of a Rumanian I didn't know, who had been arrested as a Securitate agent in Königswinter. My name and address were in his notebook. The agent was suspected of carrying out contract killings in Germany.

To 'protect' us Rolf Michaelis didn't write about the attack on himself until we had emigrated. I know from the files that this was a mistake. In the West it wasn't silence, but rather publicity that could protect you. It emerges from my file that a surreal case of 'Spying for the German Intelligence Service' was being prepared against me. Thanks to the response to my books and the literary prizes they won in Germany the plan was not implemented and I was not arrested.

Rolf Michaelis could not call us before his visit because we had no phone. You had to wait years for a telephone connection in Rumania. Nevertheless we were offered one without applying. We refused it, because we knew that a telephone would be the most practical listening post in our small flat. When we visited friends who had a telephone they always shut it in the fridge right away and put on a record. Refusing the phone didn't help, for half the material in the file that was handed over to me consists of conversations recorded in our flat.

Richard Wagner's file contains the 'Nota de analiza' dated 20 February 1985, from which it emerges that when neither of us was at home, 'Placement of special means was immediately carried out in the flat, enabling us to obtain information of operational interest'. The plan for the installation of the listening device is also in his file. They drilled through the ceiling of the flat beneath us and our floor, and placed the bugs behind the cupboards in both rooms.

The wiretap transcriptions are often full of blanks because music from records muddied the recordings. We played music because we thought the secret service used directional microphones. We never thought they would be listening to everything we said, even in the bedroom. Of course during interrogations we were continually confronted with things they could not possibly know. But given the terrible poverty and backwardness of Rumania we thought the Securitate couldn't possibly afford modern listening devices. We thought, we may well be enemies of the state, but we can't be worth all this time and effort. Despite all the fear, we remained naïve, totally mistaken about the degree of surveillance.

When my 1983 file was opened the Securitate checked the profession, place of work and political reliability of every inhabitant of our ten-storey apartment block and recorded their personal details – in all probability to recruit spies in our neighbourhood. There was a stamp for those who had not yet crossed the radar of the secret service: *'NECUNOSCUT'* (unknown).

The wiretap transcriptions are daily reports. The recorded conversations are combined, and the relevant subversive passages are played back word for word. There are question marks in the margin for unknown visitors with the instruction to find out who they are. Even the wiretap transcriptions are incomplete.

Roland Kirsch was one of our closest friends. He lived round the corner and visited us almost daily. He was an engineer in a slaughterhouse, photographed the sadness of everyday life and wrote miniature prose pieces. In 1996 his book *The Dream of the Moon Cat* was published in Germany. It was posthumously published, for he was found hanged in his flat in May 1989. Today the neighbours say there must have been a brawl in his flat, several loud voices could be heard on the night of his death. I don't believe it was suicide either. In Rumania the formalities for a burial used to take days. With suicide there was always a post-mortem. But Roland Kirsch's parents were handed all the necessary paperwork within a day. He went under the ground remarkably swiftly and without a post-mortem. And in the fat omnibus of the wiretap transcriptions there is not one single visit from Roland Kirsch. The name has been expunged, this person is not supposed to have existed.

The Tangle of Love and Betrayal

My file did answer one agonising question. Jenny came to visit me in Berlin a year after I had emigrated. After the harassment in the factory she became my closest friend. Even after I had been fired we saw each other almost every day – I trusted her. Then when I saw her passport in our kitchen in Berlin with its additional visa for France and Greece, I said to her face, 'You don't get a passport like that for nothing, what did you do for it?' Her reply: 'The secret service sent me, and I absolutely had to see you one more time.' Jenny had cancer – she is long since dead. She told us she was tasked with investigating our flat and our daily habits. When we get up and go to bed, where we go shopping and what we buy. She promised that on her return she would only report on what we agreed. She was living with us and wanted to stay for a month. By the day I grew more mistrustful. After a few days I rummaged round in her suitcase and found the phone number of the Rumanian Consulate and a copy of our house key. Since then I have lived with the suspicion that she had been set on me from the beginning, it was a friendship by proxy. As I saw from the file, when she got back she had given them detailed descriptions of the layout of our flat and our daily habits, as SURSA [source] SANDA.

But in a wiretap transcription of 21 December 1984 there is a note in the margin beside the name Jenny: 'We need to identify JENI. There is clearly a great deal of trust between the two of them.' This friendship that meant so much to me was destroyed by the Berlin visit, a woman seriously ill with cancer lured into betrayal following chemotherapy. The duplicate key made it clear that Jenny was carrying out her task surreptitiously. I had to ask her to leave our Berlin flat immediately. I had to drive away my closest friend to protect myself and my husband against her assignment. There was no way of dealing with this tangle of love and betrayal. No doubt this tangle tormented Jenny too. I have played over her visit a thousand times in my head, mourned this friendship, discovered with disbelief that Jenny even had a liaison with a Securitate officer after my departure. Today I am pleased the file shows that our closeness came from ourselves and was not engineered by the secret service, that Jenny only started spying on me after I had emigrated. We become moderate in our demands, look through what is poisoned for an uncontaminated part, however small. That my file proves the true feelings between us makes me almost happy.

The Promotion of Tradition Through Slander

After *Nadirs* was published in Germany and the first invitations
came in I was not allowed to travel. Then when invitations to literary awards started arriving the Securitate changed their strategy.

Having been unemployed up to that point, in late summer 1984
I was offered, against all expectations, a job as a teacher, and on the
first day of school I received from the director the recommendation
I needed to travel. And in October 1984 I was indeed allowed to
travel and receive literary prizes. But, as my file reveals, the intention
behind these journeys was malicious: instead of coming across as a
dissident to my teacher colleagues at school, as I had previously, I
was to be seen as a beneficiary of the regime, and in the West I was
to be suspected of being an agent.

The secret service worked enormously hard on both aspects, but
the 'agent' took precedence. Spy personnel were sent off to Germany
with a mission to slander. In the 1 July 1985 plan of action it was
happily noted that: 'as a result of several journeys abroad, the idea
was planted among certain actors in the German State Theatre of
Timisoara that CRISTINA is an agent of the Rumanian Securitate.
The West German director Alexander Montleart, who occasionally
works with the German theatre in Timisoara, has already expressed
his suspicions to Martina Olczyk of the Goethe Institute and offi-
cials of the German embassy in Bucharest.'

After I emigrated in 1987 the measures taken to 'compromise and isolate' me were ramped up. A 'Nota de analiza' of March 1989 states: 'In the action to compromise her we will work with Service D [Disinformation] by publishing certain articles abroad or sending memoranda – purporting to be from German-speaking émigrés – to certain circles and authorities that wield influence in Germany.' One of the spies allotted this task was SORIN, 'because he has the literary and journalistic background and interests required for the activities we have initiated'. On 3 July 1989 Department I/A sends a 'Raport' to the Securitate head office in Bucharest. The Rumanian writer Damian Ureche has written a letter on their instructions, denouncing Richard Wagner and me as spies. The head office is asked to approve the letter. It was to be sent to RADIO FREE EUROPE and ARD from a folk ensemble dancer who had visited Germany.

The most important 'partner' in Germany for such slanders was the Association of Banat Swabians. In 1985 the Securitate stated with satisfaction that:

'The leadership of the Association of Banat Swabians in Germany has been making negative comments about this book [*Nadirs*], together with representatives of the Rumanian embassy in Germany.' That's scandalous. Since the publication of *Nadirs,* the Association has conducted a hate campaign against me in their news-sheet, the *Banat Post.* 'Faecal language, urine prose, traitor, party whore' were the prevalent judgements of their in-house 'literary critics'. They claimed I was an informer, that I wrote *Nadirs* under orders from the Securitate.

In '*Donauschwaben*' too, another organ of the Association, the slanders go on in their 1984 Christmas edition. My use of language in *Nadirs* was 'of unparalleled vulgarity' and I myself was 'abnormal'. In addition I was the 'most valuable colleague in the Bucharest ZK Propaganda Department and other departments'. The article ends with a shameless revenge fantasy: 'To Each His Own!' – the writing above the gate of Buchenwald concentration camp.

While I sat on the concrete steps of the factory, the Association was clearly in a cosy relationship with the embassy personnel of the Ceaușescu dictatorship. I, on the other hand, would never dare set foot in that embassy, because I didn't know if I'd get out of there again. In view of these relationships with Ceaușescu's diplomats, it's not surprising that in all those years the Association of Banat Swabians has not uttered a single syllable critical of the dictatorship. Hand in glove with the regime they conducted a clearance sale of the Rumanian Germans. The bounty of up to 12,000 DM the German Federal Republic paid for every person who emigrated didn't seem to trouble the Association. Nor that this human traffic was a considerable source of hard currency for the dictatorship. The hatred directed against me and the work of slander were shared in the same spirit of agreement with the regime. I was dressed up as the enemy-in-chief, a permanent target of their Association identity. Whoever slandered me gave proof of their love of homeland. The

Association kept their traditions alive by slandering me. It seemed the word 'informer' only entered the head of the Association when it came to denouncing me. In my file it says, 'On account of her writings, which the Banat Swabians see in a bad light', members of that organisation outside Rumania had 'isolated and ridiculed' me. And: 'Our own organs also cooperated in this action through the options at our disposal abroad.'

No doubt the people planted to disrupt readings in southern Germany belong to those 'options abroad'. In the room there was a troop of my 'countrymen' whom the organisers had never seen at any other reading. They stamped their feet and demanded I read the filth from page so-and-so. They ignored requests to leave the room. They achieved their goal, the readings had to be called off.

In my file it states: 'Compromising material should also be sent to Horst Fassel at his institute address with the request that it be spread around.'

By that they mean the Danube Swabian Institute in Tübingen, whose director was Fassel at the time. And prior to that, in the eighties, he was director of the *Banat Post*.

Ernst Wichner has examined Fassel's file, 'Dosar SIE 47 310', at the Rumanian Files Authority, from which it emerges that the informant FILIP had been working for the Securitate since 1977. In 1982 he was trained for an 'external mission' in West Germany by the Department of Foreign Affairs. In 1983 he arrived in Germany on a mission to 'influence relations within the Association in line with

Rumanian interests'. In this file, in place of the code name FILIP, the real name of the spy is cited once: Horst Fassel. In 1986 he wrote in the *Banat Post*: 'the desolation that radiates out of all Herta Müller's texts has its precursors in the asphalt literature of the 1920s'. *'Asphaltliteratur'* was a phrase used by national socialist students to denounce the books they burned in 1933. To this day Fassel denies being FILIP, even though his date of birth, parents' names and wife's name are the same.

In their reports to the Rumanian secret service, spies used to ascribe to the Association in Germany an importance it never had. Despite the physical distance between them, there was clearly the same dependent relationship as between a Stasi collaborator and his commanding officer, the same pressure to work hard, the same fear of being abandoned and unmasked here in the West.

One of the most hard-working was SORIN, who ferreted out the Timisoara Authors' Group as early as 1983. An acquaintance, who examined the file of his since-deceased father, discovered from a sign in code attached to the spy's name in every report that by 1982 SORIN had submitted thirty-eight reports. In my file too, which contains over thirty names of spies, SORIN is one of the chief protagonists. In a plan of action dated 30 November 1986 it states explicitly that SORIN has been ordered to tease out what I intend to do next and what connections I have in Rumania and abroad. In Timisoara I was once visited by the features editor of the Bucharest newspaper *New Way*, who was accompanied by a Walther Konschitzky. In the wiretap transcription from that day First Lieutenant Padurariu, who was continually interrogating me, identified this visitor in the margin as: SORIN.

Like so many other spies, Walter Konschitzky commuted regularly between Rumania and Germany during the dictatorship. He emigrated before the fall of Ceauşescu and was then cultural adviser to the Association of Banat Swabians from 1992 to 1998. Since then – because this position was eliminated by the Munich head office – he continues to fulfil his function on a voluntary basis.

The Association has never been concerned about the spies in its own ranks. Since it was founded in 1950 it has created an imaginary homeland of brass bands, costume parties, pretty farmhouses and carved wooden doors. The dictatorships of Hitler and Ceauşescu were faded out as a rule. Leading members of the national socialist community in the Banat were among the founding members of the Association.

This imaginary homeland intimates to the German public a powerless, persecuted German minority in Rumania. The truth is quite different. As a percentage, just as many Germans profited from the system as Rumanians. There were German functionaries, bigwigs and headmasters too. Before, during and after my time there, Erich Pfaff was headmaster of the German Lanau Lyceum in Timisoara until he emigrated to Germany. To this day he is praised as a great guarantor of the German minority culture. Seven years after my final exam he ordered his pupil Helmuth Frauendorfer to come to his office. This was shortly before the final exam – and the headmaster was not alone. A Securitate officer was sitting next to him. The nineteen-year-old pupil was blackmailed: he wouldn't pass the exam unless he did what he was asked. An empty piece of paper was put in front of him. The nervous youth wrote down what the secret service man dictated, it was a recruitment document. He entered the headmaster's office as a schoolboy and left it an informer. He was given his next appointment with the secret service right away. His assignment: to sound out the writers in the 'Banat Action Group'. But instead of going home he came to us and reported what had happened. We advised him not to turn up for his next appointment. Then the interrogations began for him too. Now he was one of us. In all those years Frauendorfer can't be the only schoolboy to have been subjected to the honourable headmaster's lesson.

To this day the Association refuses to investigate the influence of the Securitate among their ranks on the pretext that it was all too long ago. Like the Securitate, they too hope that time will erase the traces. That is not acceptable considering their political clout in Germany. Less than ten per cent of Banat Swabian émigrés belong to their organisation, yet all those years the Association had their representatives on Broadcasting Councils and cultural institutions. After my arrival in Germany, I heard from journalists that the broadcast I did with them about the German minority during the dictatorship had caused difficulties because of the Association's intervention. In addition, for all those years they were a crucial centre for the granting of exit visas from Rumania. They tried to sabotage the exit visa of the literary critic Emerich Reichrath, whose reviews ventured beyond the minutiae of Banat life. Before I emigrated I also received letters from 'compatriots' from Germany, saying, 'You are not welcome in Germany'. In the transit hostel at Nuremberg the office of the Association was next door to the office of the German Intelligence Service. You had to run round with your docket from one office to the next, from one stamp to the next. Here and there an office wall displayed a map of Germany with its pre-1945 borders. And here and there a sign on the door proclaimed, 'I not understanding German'.

The stamp of the Association was essential to the completion of immigration formalities. I was received with the chilling sentence: 'The German air doesn't suit you.' I had a heavy cold after a night spent travelling to the border on an uncovered tractor trailer. It was February. At the German Intelligence Service behind the next door, the reception was even more brusque. Today I know why. The slander perpetrated by the Securitate unfolded: 'Did you have anything to do with the secret service over there?' My answer, 'They did with me, there's a difference,' did not impress the official. 'I'll be the judge of that. It's what I'm paid for,' he said. Then, 'If you have an assignment you can still say so now.' While all the others were able to leave this office after a few minutes with a clean bill of health, Richard Wagner and I were interrogated both separately and together for several days. Whereas my mother received her certificate of naturalisation automatically, Richard Wagner and I were told for months that 'urgent searches' needed to be done. I was in a grotesque situation. On the one hand, the office for the protection of the constitution was warning me against Securitate threats and giving me advice: don't live on the ground floor, don't accept gifts when travelling, don't leave your pack of cigarettes lying on the table, never go into a flat with strangers, buy an alarm pistol and so forth. On the other hand, my citizenship was being blocked because I was suspected of being a spy.

A few weeks before I emigrated my mother was ordered to see the village policeman early one morning. She understood from the rage in his voice and the frequent mention of my name that he was threatening her. Her Rumanian wasn't good enough to understand exactly what he was saying. Then he left the office and locked the door from outside. She was shut in there the whole day until late in the evening. After a few hours she took the bucket of water that was in the corner and used a handkerchief as a cloth, to pass the time. First she dusted the office, then she washed it down. 'What did he say when he released you?' I asked. She said, 'Absolutely nothing. He didn't even notice that his office was clean.'

It would certainly not have occurred to the village policeman to lock my mother up in the office for a whole day. This would have been on the orders of the secret service from the city. The purpose:

my mother was to get a sense of what was in store for her if she didn't emigrate with me. That through kin liability she would pay the penalty for my 'subversive activities'. She was sixty-two years old and afraid to emigrate. She wanted to wait for a while, maybe follow later. The secret service wanted everything that had anything to do with me to vanish overnight. They decided to bundle her off with me. And what they wanted, she now wanted too: a quick departure. She sold off everything she had at a loss, handed over the clean and tidy house to the state for a token price that, as she put it, 'wouldn't have paid for half of the fence'. For fear of kin liability she threw herself wholeheartedly into emigration.

The Association of Banat Swabians also made use of kin liability. In 1989 my mother had been in Berlin for two years, a vast homesickness her constant companion. A former neighbour living in Nuremberg told her that exiles from Nitzkydorf were meeting for a 'homeland day' in Augsburg. She went to Augsburg. Klaus Lanz, at that time spokesman for the Association, was the guest of honour. He took the stage, and instead of talking about homeland or being reunited, he attacked my mother about the shame of having such a daughter. My mother left the room in tears, with no chance of speaking to former neighbours and friends.

I ask myself why the German Intelligence Service suspected me, but never got on the trail of the many informers in the Association and the émigré community. No doubt the German Intelligence Service also relied on the insinuations coming from the Association.

That's why Germany is now a rich pasture for Securitate spies. When you look through the files of the Banat Authors' Group the names of numerous spies can be identified: SORIN, VOICU, GRUIA, MARIN, WALTER, MATEI and many more. They are teachers, professors, civil servants, journalists, actors, writers and some are now peaceful pensioners.

No one has ever bothered them. As far as they are concerned, the continuing debate about the Stasi since the fall of the wall can go to hell. They may all be German citizens but for the German authorities they are impenetrable. Their spying activities are extraterritorial in this country. And unlike the Stasi spies after reunification, the Securitate spies didn't lose their commanding officers. Today they are in the new Rumanian secret service.

As the files now indicate, the actor Alexander Ternovits, who amused the public with slapstick and suburban jokes and came to be known as 'Josefstadt Franzl' and 'Buju', also had a more serious occupation: under the code name MATEI he spent years spying for the Securitate. After the fall of Ceauşescu he was given honorary citizenship of Timisoara. In Rumania honour is a strange thing, burnished with a dark lustre. In 2004 in the new Rumanian democracy, the spies SORIN and Horst Fassel were decorated as 'officers' of the 'Ordinul Meritul Cultural' by then President Ion Iliescu. In free Rumania nobody feels too embarrassed to copy the investiture ceremony of the French 'Chevalier de l'Ordre' to reward Securitate spies.

And in Germany: the German parliament subsidised the work of the Association during the dictatorship, and it has subsidised their work after the fall of the dictatorship. I am not aware that any request was ever made for an investigation into the involvement of their personnel in the Rumanian dictatorship.

After the fall of Ceauşescu in 1989 I thought the campaigns of slander against me would finally be laid to rest. But they continued. I received anonymous death threats while on a scholarship at the Via Massimo in Rome in 1991. The Securitate's campaign of letters had clearly taken on a life of its own. When in 2004 I was awarded the literature prize of the Konrad Adenauer Foundation, the Foundation was not alone in receiving piles of letters with the usual calumnies. This time the campaign escalated beyond all bounds. The Presidium of the German parliament, then Prime Minister Erwin Teufel, the chairperson of the jury, Birgit Lermen, and Joachim Gauck, who was due to deliver the laudation, all received letters denouncing me as a spy, a member of the Rumanian Communist Party and a traitor. Birgit Lermen's phone rang at a quarter to twelve – Chairman of the Foundation Bernhard Vogel's at exactly midnight – and Joachim Gauck's at a quarter past midnight. Invective and threats, underlined with the Horst Wessel song. These calls went on for nights on end, until the police caught the perpetrator by intercepting the calls.

The Double and Her Own Paths

In my file I am two distinct people. One is called CRISTINA, an enemy of the state, who must be taken on. To compromise this CRISTINA a double is created in the forgery workshop of Department D (Disinformation) with all the ingredients that would be most damaging to me – hardened Communist, ruthless agent, party member, which, unlike many functionaries of the Association, I never was.

I had to live with this double everywhere I went. Not only was she sent after me, she rushed on ahead of me. Although from the very beginning I only ever wrote against the dictatorship, the double follows her own paths to this day. She has become independent. The dictatorship is over and done with these last twenty years, but the double still flits about. How much longer?

The King Bows Down and Kills

I am often asked why the king comes up so often in my texts and the dictator so rarely. The word 'king' sounds soft. I am often asked why the barber comes up so often in my texts. The barber measures hair, and hair measures life.

In the novel *Back Then The Fox Was the Hunter* a child asks the barber:

When does the man who has thrown the cat away die? The barber put a handful of sweets in his mouth. When enough hair has been cut off a man to fill a sack, a sack full to the brim, he said. When the sack is as heavy as the man, the man dies. I put the hair of each man in a sack until the sack is full to the brim, said the barber. I don't weigh the hair on scales. I weigh it by eye.[11]

The barber, the hair and the king came together long before I knew the dictator and before I started to write.

Still alive the king looked like a dog and a calf
his crown stuck to him in death
like a melon of bile
angels prowling under his hair like summer rains
between the stalks of corn each
a guardian of the king

There was no asphalt road leading to the remote village where I grew up, only bumpy dirt tracks. But the king found his way there, otherwise he would not have met me. He was nothing to do with the kings in the fairy tales. I had no books of fairy tales. He was made up of real things, of lived experience. He came from my grandfather's chess set, and the chess set was linked to his hair. During the First World War my grandfather was a soldier, he was sent to a prisoner of war camp, and there he carved a chess set.

The prisoner of war's hair fell out in clumps and the regimental barber treated his scalp with the sap of crushed leaves. The barber had a great passion: whenever and wherever he could he played chess. He had taken his chess set off to war with him. But in the turmoil of the front the barber lost seven chessmen. In a game they had to be replaced with bits of bread crust, birds' feathers, twigs or pebbles. As my grandfather's hair grew back thicker and darker than ever after a few weeks of treatment, he wondered how he could thank the barber. Inside the confines of the camp he noticed two trees, one of chalk-white wood and the other of dark red wood. From these he carved the missing chess pieces and gave them to the barber. That's how it started, he said to me. The carving had brought him too close to the chessmen, he said, it felt like a loss that he didn't know their function on the board. He learned to play chess. Not only did this alleviate the tedium of long days of waiting, it was something you could hold on to. While playing, head and fingers were in, if not the real world, then a version of it. One lived one's way out of the savage present to the memory of a former home, then on to the hope of returning home soon. Unawares, one had slid into the chessmen. The time of the game carried you along, he said, you didn't have to endure it in all its emptiness. After his release my grandfather returned to the village, and as with the regimental barber, chess had become his passion.

Carving those seven chessmen and the slow passage of time, he said, forced him to keep working with his hands. There was enough wood in the trees, and he carved a complete chess set for himself. First the pawns, he said, because he was a peasant before the war and he wanted to get home and be a peasant again.

When he told me the story, he had for some time owned a decent shop-bought chess set. I was allowed to play with the hand-carved one, which had four pieces missing. Of all his chessmen I liked the two kings best, the chalk-white and the dark red. The wood had become old and soiled with time, greyish white and dark brown, like parched, rain-drenched earth. All the pieces were cracked and wobbly, and no two were alike. Each piece of fresh-cut wood dried out in its own way. The most lopsided were the kings, frail as they were with pot bellies and hunchbacks. They wobbled, for the crowns on their heads were askew and far too large. For decades my grandfather played chess every weekend. But once all his chess friends had died one after another he played cards on Sundays for company. Then he had another stroke of luck. Year in year out, every few weeks, he used to visit his sister, married to a man from the neighbouring village. And on one of his visits to this village he met a 'serious' chess partner, as he put it. From then on he took the train to this village every Wednesday to play chess. I was often allowed to go with him. Just as only Germans lived in our village, so only Hungarians lived in the next village. My great-aunt's husband was Hungarian and a carpenter. And the serious chess partner was Hungarian too. As he played chess my grandfather could indulge two passions at once, for his second passion was speaking Hungarian. I was encouraged to go with him so I could learn Hungarian as he played chess.

Grandfather's brother-in-law, the carpenter, wore a smock of sawdust, brown fabric was visible only under the arms. His beret too was of sawdust, and his temples and his ears, and he had a thick sawdust moustache. He made furniture, floors, doors, windows, prams that could be shaded with wooden blinds, he made small

items like clothes hangers, chopping boards, wooden spoons and –
he made coffins.

After the fall of the Berlin wall the German press often published
examples of the GDR's official language prescriptions. Spoken aloud
and correctly, these word monsters became unintentionally funny –
botched in their construction, bungled in content. Christmas-tree
angels were called 'year-end winged creatures', the little flags that
were brandished in front of the rostrums were called 'waveable ele-
ments', and shops selling drink were known as 'drink bases'. Two of
these GDR words seemed familiar to me, reminded me of visits to
my carpenter uncle. One was the coffin, which in GDR German
was called 'earth furniture'. The other was the name of the Stasi
department in charge of the feast days and funeral days of the bigwigs, it was called 'Department of Joy and Sorrow'. 'Year-end
winged creature', to avoid the word 'angel'. 'Waveable element'to
avoid 'little flag', for such a diminutive would have been an insult to
the flag. 'Drink bases' gives the shop greater military power, maybe
the bigwigs slaked their 'thirst for freedom' from a bottle. With
these concepts a clumsy, tone-deaf ideology had created word cari-
catures. To my ears 'earth furniture' and the Stasi's 'Department of
Joy and Sorrow' didn't sound at all funny. You can hear fear of
death in these word formations. For death could not be tamed by
high office in the state, it broke through the boundary between the
Nomenklatura and the foot soldiers. The collective eternity of the
ruling clique was clearly not indifferent to the knowledge of death,

to which we are all subject, along with the 'normal folk'. They cringed before this single weak point of the power they wielded, which made no distinction between socialist heroes and enemies of the state, took each of us to task in the greatest privacy, and without Marx and Lenin, let alone Honecker and Mielke, able to help. In the Marxist linguistic creation 'earth furniture' instead of coffins, God is so to speak within and without, he is both denied and taken into consideration. It's not a question of 'resurrection', but nevertheless a kind of consolation is projected on to death, an afterlife. You are given your earth furniture and you live in your room under the earth. Viewed in this light it is only logical that, embalmed, Lenin is entitled to a villa in Red Square, whereas ordinary people in the cemetery must make do with bachelor quarters.

The Hungarian carpenter with the sawdust smock put the words 'earth furniture' into practice without knowing any GDR German. In line with the pragmatics of his work, the coffin in his house became a piece of furniture that went under the ground when someone was laid out in it. All his wooden creations were scattered as space in the workshop dictated: a finished pram beside, above, below or even inside a finished coffin. There in the workshop the wood revealed all the stations between birth and death. Like a pauper, the passage of life lay there full of wooden spoons, chopping boards and coat hangers. The coffins looked so natural amongst cupboards, bedside tables, beds, chairs and tables, truly furniture for the earth. Nothing was lying low, objects were present, more real than words could evoke. They needed no foolish talk of life and death, they were what was needed for life and death.

The carpenter could do anything. In my eyes he made the world. I understood that it is not made of shifting skies and grassy corn fields, but of unchanging wood. He could lay down wood every-where against the fleeing seasons, against the bare and the grassy seasons of the earth. Here was a waxworks of dying days made of smoothly polished, angular material. A clarity in subdued colours, from dirty white through honey-yellow to dark brown. Colours which didn't shift, but grew a shade darker, rather than fluttering as landscape and dissipating. They had a mute quality, a calm confi-dence. They didn't frighten me, when I grasped them they remained so still their calmness spread through me. As the seasons out there jostled and finally consumed each other, these coffins in the work-shop did not give offence to the flesh. They took their time and they waited. For the dead they were merely the final bed to carry them away. The carpenter had a sewing machine too and sewed death pil-lows for the coffins. 'White damask,' he said, 'filled with plane shadows, fit for a king.' The long wooden curls that fell from the plane were not called 'wood shavings' but 'plane shadows'. I like this phrase. I liked the idea that the pillows of the dead did not contain foliage, straw or sawdust – rather the shadow contained in the wood of the living treetops that fell out when the wood was cut. Alexandru Vona writes in his novel *The Bricked Up Windows*: 'If we want to experience the truth we must discover the words and phrases which don't concern us that have wormed their way among the others.'[12] For me 'plane shadows' is one such phrase.

The plane shadows rustled and smelled bitter. While my grandfather played chess on the veranda, I made wigs out of the short plane shadows in the workshop. From the long squiggles I made belts, mufflers and shawls. There were golden letters in a big box, and they gave off a piercing smell of varnish. The carpenter made up the name of the departed from these letters and stuck them on the coffin lid. I made myself rings, necklaces and ear pendants. Today the plane shadows and letters would scare me. At that time I had seen so many dead people I had known well when they were alive, their voices and their gait. For years I had known what they wore and ate, how they turned over the soil, how they danced. Then one day they lay in the coffin, they were the same but motionless and intent on the last visit. Only once more did they wish to be important, swaying to music through the village in the carved coach, a veritable travelling veranda. God had claimed his material back from them, the region had consumed them along with the season. I scarcely thought about them when I was adorning myself with the golden letters. I admired the carpenter uncle, because he ensured that the dead had bed covers with their name in golden letters and damask pillows full of plane shadows, that they were carried off. Many coffins stood dense and upright against the wall, like fences. Many lay flat on the ground, filled with plane shadows. Not once while I was visiting was a name of golden letters stuck on, a pillow sewed and filled with plane shadows, a coffin sold. At midday the carpenter's wife brought the food and placed it in the plane shadows of a coffin, to keep the pot warm.

In the workshop were plane shadows and white damask cushions fit for a king, and my grandfather frowned and ground his teeth over the chessboard. Sometimes his king was checkmate and sometimes his partner's. And on the short journey home on the late train the sky had the garish colour of evening that's unlike anything else. The moon hung like a horseshoe or an apricot, on the roofs the weathercocks travelled in the direction opposite to the train, like so many chess pieces. Some resembled the king. The next day the chickens in the grass wore crowns but not combs. Every week on Wednesdays and Saturdays I had to slaughter a chicken. I did it like any other job, competently and without feeling, like peeling potatoes or dusting, like a job you've spent your life doing. It was woman's work. Not to torment a chicken, not to see blood, that didn't exist. With men it did, apart from while shaving. And rarely with women, who – so it was said – were good for nothing. Later on I was maybe not up for it, back then I was up for it.

My dreams were jumbled: I cut the chicken up, its stomach a casket full of chess pieces, red and blue, rather than white and black. They are dry and hard, their clatter must have echoed when the chicken was running through the grass. I take the chess pieces out of the stomach and place them in two rows by colour. There is only one king, he staggers, bows. He is green, and as he bows he turns red. I hold him in my hand and feel his heart beating. He is afraid and so I bite into him. Inside he is yellow and soft, his flesh sweet like an apricot. I eat him.

Every object had its king, and when they appeared the kings winked at the other kings. The kings did not abandon their objects, but they knew each other, met in my head and belonged there together. They were a divided king, always seeking out new material they could inhabit: the wooden king in the chess set, the metal king in the weathercock, the meat king in the chicken. On inspection, the material the objects were made of was subject to the kind of intensity that triggers a disconnection in the head. The normal state of things exploded, its substance reduced to servitude. Hierarchies developed between equal objects, and even more so between me and them. I had to stand up to the comparisons I had initiated, and I could only lose. Compared to wood, metal or a feather dress, skin is the most ephemeral of materials. I was inevitably dependent on the sometimes good, sometimes evil power of the king.

the rooster lives in the feather house
a boulevard in the leaf house
a hare in the fur house
a lake in the water house
in the corner house the sentinel
pushes a suicide from the balcony

over the elder tree
in the paper house the statement
in the hair knot a lady

The text of this collage is a late response to the cobbled together king of the village. And the town king has long been at work with the corner house of the patrol and the murder, which was falsified on paper as suicide in the statement. He is a state king. He haggles at the point where life and death cross, he throws those who have become troublesome secretly out of the window, under trains or cars, from river bridges, hangs them with a rope, poisons them — stages the killing as suicide. He has people trying to escape across the border ripped apart by trained bloodhounds, he leaves them lying there for the peasants to find half rotted in the fields at harvest time. He has those who try to escape across the Danube hunted down by boats and ground to powder by the propellers. Food for fishes and gulls. This one knows, but can never prove, and it happens every day. A person's disappearance, followed by silence, relatives and friends with eyes all too wide. The town king doesn't reveal his weaknesses, he staggers, you think he bows down, but he bows down and kills.

with reason my king says
I love you all
his angry royal hound

wears a uniform of shimmering grass
and a wavy iron buckle
at night the snowy lantern leaps and breathes
as if someone loved to death
lay at dawn in the belly of a dog

The village king 'bowed down a little', he staggered as the region staggered. We lived in the region that was consuming itself, until it consumed you too, until you died. The town king was the first to carry out the latter part of the sentence: 'the king bows down and kills'. The town king's tool is fear. Not the imagined village fear, but planned, coldly administered fear that shatters the nerves. After I arrived in town from the fringes of the village the asphalt became a carpet upon which, instead of the waxworks of death, state-planned death slithered round your ankles: repression. In the first few years I could see it everywhere. It affected people I didn't know personally. I feared it in general, lived too close not to be aware of it but too far to understand the damage it was doing. In those early days it ran beside me, never through me. I felt a great deal of sympathy for those who had just encountered it, spontaneous compassion that held me for a while then dissipated. Standing there with crooked fingers, pressing fingernails into palms till the pain comes, biting your lip as you watch someone you don't know being arrested, beaten and kicked in broad daylight. Then walking straight ahead, gums dry, skin on the neck prickling, as if stomach and legs had been pumped full of putrid air. Feeling that queasy guilt at not being able to prevent something that is happening to others and the seedy good fortune that the punishment has not been visited upon you. It could have struck anyone who was watching, everything other than breathing was forbidden. Wherever you looked there were untold grounds for arrest.

Then in the next few years I did have friends who were tailed and regularly interrogated, whose flats were searched, whose manuscripts were seized, who were banned from studying and arrested. What I had initially experienced as an oppressive atmosphere became real fear. My friends were tortured and I knew precisely where and how. We spent whole days talking about it, caught between humour and fear, foolhardy and on edge, we looked for ways out, but there were none, and reneging on our own actions was unthinkable. The reprisals edged into my life. Several years later they edged beneath my skin – I was asked to spy on my colleagues in the factory and I refused. And everything I knew from friends about interrogations, house searches and death threats happened to me. I was used to reflecting on this, how the next interrogation, the next day's work, the next street corner laid traps.

Aware that eyes made wide by fear and a disconnection in the head cause all words to flee, both written and spoken, I nevertheless had to add something in writing upon the death of two friends. Just as I once sought words for milk thistle back in the large, bright green valley, so I sought out words to describe the fear we all experienced. I wanted to show how friendship looks when there is no knowing whether one will be alive this evening, tomorrow morning, next week:

Because we were afraid, Edgar, Kurt, Georg and I met every day. We sat together at a table, but our fear stayed locked within each of our heads, just as we'd brought it to our meetings. We laughed a lot, to hide it from each other. But fear always finds an out. If you control your face, it slips into your voice. If you manage to keep a grip on your face and your voice, as if they were dead wood, it will slip out through your fingers. It will pass through your skin and lie there. You can see it lying around on objects close by. We could see whose fear was where, because we had known each other so long. Often we couldn't stand each other, because we were all we had.[13]

The interrogator asked me contemptuously, 'Who do you think you are.' It wasn't a question, so I took the opportunity to answer: 'I am a human being like you.' That was necessary and important to me, his behaviour was so overbearing that he seemed to have forgotten that fact. During the more turbulent phases of the interrogations he called me a piece of shit, a piece of filth, a parasite, a bitch. When he was calmer, a whore or an enemy. During the more harmless phases of the interrogations I was there to fill up his working hours, the rag you squeeze to demonstrate your diligence and competence. He often practised destroying people on me, because there were hours left in the working day, he kept me there, chewed over ironically or cynically everything that had been said in a rage a thousand times. I had to stay so the clock didn't tick on into the void, so he didn't have to fall back on his own resources. After each outburst of rage he rehearsed his hounding of people on me, to keep his relaxed, casual manner sharp. There was a routine in all his moods. The childish question, 'What is my life worth?' became obsolete. Such a question can only come from inside. When asked from outside you become recalcitrant. You love your life out of sheer obstinacy. Every day acquires a value, you learn to love life. You tell yourself you are alive. You want to live right now. And that's enough, it's more meaning of life than you think. It's tried and tested meaning of life, as valid as breathing itself. This lust for life that grows inside despite all external circumstances is also a king. A recalcitrant king, I know him well. That's why I've never mentioned him in words, kept his name hidden. I came up with 'heart-beast' so I could address him, not say his name out loud. Only many years later, when those times were far enough behind me, did I move from 'heart-beast' to 'king'.

the king bows down
and as night comes
from the factory roof
two shoes shine into the river

neon pale and inside out
as one kicks teeth in
and the other ribs to pulp
and in the morning they're gone
and the crab apple is witty
and the maple blushes
and the stars in the sky
explode like popcorn
and the king bows down
and kills

The rhyme from the language of my village drew me to the king from the start: I used to rhyme *'allein – wenig – König'* when I was with the cows in the valley: *'alleenig – wenig – Kenig'* (alone – little – king). That rhyme and the king from my grandfather's chess set. From the village dialect I know rhymes on wall hangings, in prayers, in saws about the weather. As a child I took them seriously, as an adolescent in the city I ridiculed them. At school we used to flog Goethe's and Schiller's ballads to death for months on end. Mindlessly reeled off without a thought in our heads, the emphasis on the last syllable. In our heads it was the same rhythm as beating a carpet: 'through the night dark and drear/The father it is, with his infant so dear' or 'From visions of disastrous love/Leonora starts at dawn of day/How long, my Wilhelm, wilt thou rove?/Does death or falsehood cause thy stay?' The rhyming poems put out by the party were even worse: 'I love the land vouchsafed me hereabout/and all who labour, every man and boy/and the mother tongue that sings out/for peace and socialism, strength and joy'. The rhyme staggered along, it was impossible to get the carpet-beating rhythm going. If you declaimed six or seven verses in a row it sounded like potholes in your head. I was repulsed by rhymes. It wasn't till later that I discovered the restrained rhymes of Theodor Kramer and Inge Müller. I sensed gentle, vulnerable rhythms, as if this style of rhyming made the breath beat against the temples. I became obsessed with these poems, knew dozens of them by heart without ever having committed them to memory. They had my own life in mind, they spoke directly to me. I liked them so much I didn't dare take a close look at how they were constructed. To this day I believe that even close examination will not reveal the special quality of these two authors. Then I began cutting words out of newspapers. At first that led me past the rhymes. It started as a way of keeping in touch with friends during my frequent travels, of putting something personal in the envelope rather than postcards of places seen through the jingoistic lens of a photographer. While reading the newspaper on a train I stuck a fragment of a photograph and some words together on a white card, or perhaps one or two sentences: 'the stubborn word SO' or: 'If there really is a place, then it touches longing'. The amazement created by loose newspaper words resulted in rhymes. I have long cut words out at home. They seemed to lie indiscriminately on the table. I looked at them, and it was remarkable how many rhymed. Trusting the rhymes of Theodor Kramer and Inge Müller, I accepted those rhymes for which I had done nothing, which had come together by chance on the table's surface. The words had got to know each other because they had to share the space they lay on. I couldn't chase them away so I discovered the taste for rhyming.

From the very beginning I could not allow the word 'king' to remain in any text of mine. I was fixated on it, I cut the word 'king' from every text in which it appeared. I once counted them on the table, there were twenty-four kings lying next to each other before I allowed the first one to appear in a text. The rhymes surfaced when he was allowed into the text. It turned out you could get the better of the king through rhymes. You can run rings round him. The rhyme forces him back into the racing heartbeat that he causes. The rhyme causes smooth swerves in the distress the king has brought about. The rhyme causes a stir and imposes discipline at the same time. The whole line can change step, enter into complicity with other lines. With rhymes you can brush them against the grain, hide them in the middle of sentences and watch as they absorb that which they reveal. And at the end of the sentence you can give them weight and space, yet not emphasise them while reading aloud, hiding them in the voice.

The king was in my head since I was a child. He was present in things. Even if I had never written a word, he would have been there to get a grip on the new complications I encountered as a familiar if malevolent leitmotif. Wherever the king made an appearance you could expect no rest. Nevertheless he sorted life out, dealt wordlessly with the chaos when it went beyond what could be said. The king was always a lived word, there was no getting the better of him through talk. I have spent a lot of time with the king, and during that time fear was either an incidental or an overwhelming presence.

In contrast to the lived 'king', 'heart-beast' is a written phrase. It cropped up on paper as substitute for the king while I was writing, because I needed a phrase to describe lust for life while in mortal fear, a phrase that I didn't have back then, when I lived in fear. I wanted something as double-edged as the king. It had to contain timidity as well as despotism. And it had to go inside the body, the guts, an inner organ, freighted with the body around it. I wanted to address the unpredictable, that is present in every human being, in me just as in the powerful. Something that doesn't know itself. It's tame or wild according to the dictates of fate and our own wishes.

On my first New Year's Eve in Germany the king was suddenly standing there in the middle of the party after midnight. The guests were starting to pour lead. I watched as the molten lead from the teaspoon hissed into the cold water and solidified into an unpredictable shape. That's exactly how it is with the king, I thought, and how it should be with the heart-beast. I was asked to pour my lead ghost for the New Year, and I didn't dare. I withdrew from the whole business with a laugh so no one suspected the reason, not a good idea to pour hot lead if your nerves are shot. The other lead pourers were driven by a lively imagination. I had reflected far too much. I refused to pour the lead out of fear that the lead ghost might cut me off from the heart-beast, might harass and paralyse me all year if I sought to hold the heart-beast. But that may be the extension of the same problem, I thought: they all want to judge by the object that crawls from my spoon how mentally shot I am, and what great pains I take to formulate my inner state with the words 'heart-beast'. In *The Woman in the Window*, an oppressive film directed by Fritz Lang, someone says, 'You get into situations you hadn't bargained for just a few minutes before.' I had bargained for something, for a lead pouring game to show me what I didn't want to deal with.

The king followed me, first from the village to the city, then from Rumania to Germany, as a reflection of what could never be clarified for me. He personalised the scale of things. If in the confusion inside my head no word comes to mind, to this day I say: here comes the king.

I was already in Germany when one of my friends was found hanged in his flat. In the country where I had to leave friends behind, yet again the king had bowed down and killed. Roland Kirsch was killed, a civil engineer who was twenty-eight years old, who spoke little and softly, who didn't make a song and dance about himself, who wrote poems, took photographs, and unlike others, who didn't terminate our friendship, not while I was an enemy of the state in Rumania nor following my departure. He sent postcards to me in Berlin, knowing fully what the risks were. I wanted him to let our friendship lie fallow, not expose himself to danger, I was afraid for him. In the midst of this fear I was even more pleased when his postcards arrived – they were a sign of life. His last card, sent a couple of weeks before his death, was a black-and-white photo – a street we often used to walk down. It had changed a lot since my departure, tram tracks had been laid. The new tracks were already overgrown with waist-high wild carrots. They blossomed with filigree white bird's nests. They showed me the danger my friend was in, that my path had led me away from there, that our closeness had been ripped apart, the spontaneity of our friendship confiscated, for we could never be direct when writing, we had to scour the words in their niches while reading to discover which word meant what. The image of our separation in the wild carrots. I thought perhaps all plants that watch the futility of human beings turn into wild carrots. On the reverse of the card was a single sentence in tiny script: 'Sometimes I have to bite my finger to feel I still exist.'

Soon thereafter, he no longer existed. That sentence weighs heavier than its words can say. And it leads to a place where words can no longer endure, not even the words one has to use to quote him. It's not about the sentence, after all, but about the human being. And no human being should be so encased in a sentence as he must be in that one, because he was forced into it. As with the sentence, so with the day of his death: the first of May, the great Socialist day of celebration, 'International Workers' Day'. On International Workers'

Day a dictator obsessed with tormenting people and erecting monumental structures rid himself of a civil engineer. The king had his hands round my throat when I received the news. How does it feel, when you are sitting at home late in the evening, there is a knock at the door, you open it and you are hanged. The neighbours now say they heard voices yelling that night. No one went to help. A postmortem was refused. The king didn't want anyone to look at his cards. The official statement on the death certificate declares: suicide. The question remains: did they set out to hang him. Did he defend himself and was then forced to put his head in the noose. Or did he die at their hand that night under interrogation or torture, and they didn't know what to do with the corpse, and so hanged him. Did they do it deliberately, or out of fear when their plan went awry, out of scorn or simply for their amusement. Were the murderers full-time secret service men or hired hands, or else criminals who had been blackmailed.

Perhaps because of the refusal to do a post-mortem, the shock of this death brought back like an echo a reverse case from my childhood, the mulberry king from the village. He had undoubtedly hanged himself, and the post-mortem was carried out. He was in the final phase of cancer and was given penicillin injections, because the doctor had no morphine. He could stand the ravages of pain no longer and made an appointment with death. In his back yard was a mulberry tree, and under it a ladder. Every year his chickens were trained to sleep in the tree. Each evening they climbed the ladder to the top of the tree, sat down to sleep in rows on the branches. At daybreak they climbed down the ladder to the yard. The dead man's daughter said he had got very close to the chickens while training them, which lasted weeks. They were not unsettled when he hanged himself from their tree. There was no fluttering, no cries, not a sound in the yard that night. Around three in the morning the daughter said she wanted to see how he was. His pyjamas lay on the bed without him, the cupboard was open and the clothes hanger that held his good suit was empty. Her first thought was that he had gone to the yard to ease his pain. But why in his Sunday suit. She dared to go outside. Moonlight lifted the entire yard out of darkness. As ever the chickens sat up in the mulberry tree. The white ones, particularly the white ones, she said, were gleaming like porcelain in a shop window. And he was hanging from a branch below them. The hanged man was my neighbour. Countless times, when I saw that tree in the years that followed, the disconnection in my head kicked off, I kept repeating the same sentence to myself: he and his chickens used the same ladder.

The penicillin doctor did not reproach himself. He had the nerve to doubt that it was suicide, insisted on a post-mortem. He stripped the dead man of the dignity of his good suit, played the great expert and conducted the post-mortem on a hot summer's day on a butcher's block in the middle of the yard beside the ladder up to the mulberry tree. That's why the lid had to go straight on the coffin when the cut up dead man was laid to rest in the best room of his house. Still I imagined I could see the blue-black stripe around his neck, indigo blue like the mulberries out on the tree. Like the comb of the chicken, the stripe round his neck was now his crown. The dead man had served notice on his flesh, he had moved on to a different matter, stiller, merged with the flesh of the fruit. With the dark ring round his neck and his good suit he had turned himself into the biggest mulberry ever to be found on a tree. He entered the earth as the mulberry king.

In Alexandru Vona's novel *The Bricked Up Windows* the mulberry king made an unexpected appearance. He's a woman whose necklace anticipates the blue stripe round the neck from hanging. Still the mulberry king of my childhood squats in her neck.

As she drank the glass my father had handed her, I noticed on her thick neck the black velvet ribbon, from which hung a locket. A month later, we learn that father was not mistaken. I asked him how she had killed herself. In fact my question was a mere formality, for with the black choker before my eyes, I knew that she had hanged herself [. . .] Perhaps the taut choker (if you had worked a finger under it she would have suffocated) was why she held herself so upright.[14]

After my friend was hanged I could never see nooses in the same light again. I avoid them to this day, in buses I don't hold on to the hand straps. If a coat is hanging on the hall stand, for a split second, like a finger snapping in my head, there are feet below it, then they are gone. In a station concourse I once bought a postcard which showed the different kinds of knot used in tying a necktie. The various knots are quite clearly nooses that go around the neck under the collar. It was madness. When I bought it I imagined I would be able to defy the whole range of knots. I wanted to be rid of the terror, to stare at it until it no longer had a hold on me. I couldn't send the card to anyone. I shoved it under a pile of paper in a drawer at home. It has lain there for years. I can't use it and I can't get rid of it.

Just as the power elite staged their murders as suicide, when it came to their own they did the reverse: the suicides of the bigwigs were portrayed as accidents. Across the entire country the cliques of high- and middle-rank functionaries were obliged to, or were desperate to, imitate the greatest hunter, Ceauşescu. So hunting became the sport of functionaries, a sort of party activity in the forest. Even the bigwigs from the tiniest backwater went hunting. When one of the bigwigs in Timisoara, weary of life, had lain in wait in the forest not for a deer but for the moment he was alone then promptly put a bullet in his brain, the local newspaper, the *Paper House*, reported that he had been torn from this world by a tragic hunting accident. My friends and I knew a student whose father had been involved in that hunt. Because we lived with death threats and had to view our lifespan as controlled by the state, we derived a great deal of bitter humour from such news. My civil engineer friend, who was hanged four or five years later and whose death is now on record as suicide, had this to say about the 'hunting accident': 'The hunter aims at the deer, so the deer must have run across the roof of the hunter's mouth.' We cracked jokes about the 'palate deer'. These jokes cried out to be embellished, one led to another: 'A bird in the hand is better than a deer in the mouth', or 'Rather the village church than a bug under the cupboard, and rather a bug under the cupboard than the lid on the coffin.' We all added something, these improvised tales gathered a mosaic of sporadic images, people trying to outdo themselves and each other, spontaneous group poetry, sarcastic, full throttle, to tame the fear we felt. This dynamic evolved because each one of us had to take what had been said a step further into the absurd. The end result began like any good German fairy tale: 'Once upon a time there was', and it continued, 'Once upon a time there was, as it never was'. That's how all Rumanian fairy tales began. Even this classic Rumanian beginning to a fairy tale, which referred to the woefully cobbled together lies of the regime, was reason enough for gleeful laughter. Then we progressed in stages: 'Once upon a time there was, as it was. And that was back when it was, but it never was. Once upon a time there was, it didn't matter how it was. And there was a time, but it is not known which time it was, but it never was. Once upon a time on a hunt, which was the last time, there was a hunter among hunters, of whom it is not known how many they were. When there was no other hunter far and wide, although it is not known how far and how wide, apart from the one, of whom it is not known which one of how many he was . . .' It was important that the relativisms escalate, go to extremes, the sentences become labyrinths. At some point in the course of this interweaving, the roof of the hunter's mouth would run, tender, pink and bare, across the hard forest floor, encounter a deer, sprout horns and pelt and look just like the deer and get mistakenly shot by its owner. Then we said: 'The palate and the deer resembled each other as one forest resembles another, as a tree or branch or leaf resembles another, as a flag or a pea resembles another, as one comrade resembles another.' We had long horizons, a kind of sovereign territory, with our labyrinthine sentences, we laid down so many trails and detours that our heads were spinning.

I've invented these sentences, because I've long since forgotten the ones from those days. But they might well have been like that. The gap between fear of death and lust for life provoked the king. There was lust for life in our group poetry. Crass jokes as an imaginary dismantling of the regime. We gave ourselves courage, because those we were laughing at could have ended our lives any day they chose. These comic tales we assembled were a cheerfully won, stolen merriment. The bugs we laughed about were in the room, someone was listening in. And at some point, when you had forgotten your contribution and that of the others after who knows how many interrogations, the interrogators took back the stolen time. Every single word was weighed, and the whole thing translated badly into

Rumanian. There was no question of humour now. We were each confronted in turn by the interrogators with the secret service analysis of our 'pronouncements against the state'. This went on for half a day at a time, until your own head no longer knew who it belonged to. When we were finally allowed to go, we sat down together again to discuss how best to conduct ourselves, how to deny what one had said without incriminating others. What bothered me was that the bad translations into Rumanian had made our stories no less dangerous politically, but had mangled their literary quality. It was as if the poetry had evaporated. At the interrogation, as everything came back through the endless chewing over of the material, one felt a sudden desire to make up for the poetry that was lost. The instinct to replace the poetic losses had to be suppressed. It would have been tantamount to self-incrimination.

At every interrogation, when he felt he had me checkmate, the interrogator would say to me in triumph: 'You see, everything is connected.' Without knowing why, he was right. He had no idea of all the things that were connected in my head against him. That he was sitting at a big polished desk and I was at a small table made of filthy, badly planed wood. 'You see', yes, I could see the table's surface covered in scores from the interrogations of other people I knew nothing of, not even if they were still alive. Because I had to look at him for hours on end, the interrogator became the king in the course of every interrogation. For his bald patch he could have used my grandfather's regimental barber. For his calves too, which gleamed white between the hem of his trousers and the top of his socks, with not a hair in sight. Inside his head things were ganging up against me. But in my head completely different things were ganging up: just as there was a king who bowed in the chess set, the interrogator was a king who kills. During one of the first interrogations on a summer afternoon, the plane shadows came into play. The glass in the windows was shimmering in the sun. Wavy stripes of white light fell to the floor and climbed up the interrogator's trouser leg as he crossed the room. I wanted him to stumble, wanted the stripes to sneak inside his shoes and kill him through the soles of his feet.

And a few weeks later the king came not just into his missing hair, but into my own hair. Again curls of sunlight lay on the floor between our two desks. Longer than usual, snaking brightly, they crawled back and forth because there was a high wind outside. The interrogator was pacing up and down, he was nervous, the plane shadows were so restless he couldn't keep his eyes off them. Between my real but motionless presence and the plane shadows, which were there only as a reflection, but which skipped around crazily, he lost control. He screamed as he paced back and forth. I was expecting a slap. He raised his hand, but then he took a stray hair from my shoulder and was about to let it fall to the floor from two outstretched fingers. I don't know why I suddenly said, 'Please put the hair back. It belongs to me.' He touched me again very slowly on the shoulder, his arm seeming to move in slow motion, shook his head, walked to the window through the curls of sunlight, stared at the tree then burst out laughing. It wasn't till he laughed that I could see my shoulder out of the corner of my eye. He really had replaced the hair, precisely where it had lain before. The king's laughter was no use to him. He hadn't been prepared for the hair episode. He had come too far out of the saddle, made a fool of himself. And I felt such a dumb sense of satisfaction, as if I had him in the palm of my hand. The destruction he had trained for depended on a routine, he had to stick to it. Any improvisation was a risk. Not a real risk, one I had dreamed up, but by my foolish calculation it counted.

The hair and the barber always had to do with the king. My friends and I used to spread hairs around the flat before we went out. We placed them on door knobs, cupboard handles, on manuscripts in drawers, on books in the shelves – they were clever signs because they were inconspicuous, they showed if objects had been moved around in our absence, if the secret police had been there. 'By a hair's breadth' and 'thin as a hair' were no longer sayings for us, but habit.

There is a passage in the novel *The Land of Green Plums*:

Our heart-beasts fled like mice. They sloughed off their skins and disappeared into nothingness. When we spoke in rapid succession, they hung in the air a little longer. When you write, don't forget to put the date, and always put a hair with the letter, said Edgar. If there isn't one, we'll know the letter's been opened. Single hairs, I thought to myself, crisscrossing the country on trains. A dark hair of Edgar's, a light one of mine. A red one of Kurt or of Georg.[15]

After a whole flock of secret service men had searched my friend Rolf Bossert's flat and made off with all his manuscripts and letters, Bossert picked up a pair of scissors, went to the bathroom, stood in front of the mirror and cut fistfuls of hair from his head and his beard. This was shortly before he left for Germany. Seven weeks later we realised that this wild attack on his hair with the scissors was a first attempt to lay a hand on himself. Seven weeks later, having been in Germany for six weeks, he threw himself from the window of the transit hostel. With men even more than with women, the hairstyle was often a political indicator. It showed the hold the state had on a person, the degree to which they were oppressed.

All the men the state had claimed, whether for a while or forever, had shaved heads: soldiers, prisoners, children in the orphanages. And all those schoolchildren who had been up to no good. The length of the children's hair was checked every day in schools – the back of the neck had to be shaved halfway up the head, with a finger's breadth between earlobes and hair. And not just in junior schools, in the secondary schools too. At university students were also instructed not to show up with long hair. There was the barber for men and the hairdresser for women. It was unthinkable that women and men should go to the same establishment. The king insisted on maintaining control by dividing the sexes.

Even when I look at my childhood photos, the king is bowing. From each photo I can tell how my mother felt that morning, as she combed my hair. Photographers rarely came to the village, and I can no longer recall how it happened that I was photographed against a wall and a flower bed in the churchyard on a snowy path in the middle of the village. The photos give no information at all about me, but a great deal about my mother. For they contain two or three flashbacks to the way she was. The first: the centre parting is crooked and both plaits have been twisted high up behind the ears – that means my father was only mildly drunk the night before. On those days my mother combed my hair stoically, keeping her thoughts to herself, her fingers engaged in a practised routine. The marriage was going reasonably well, life was bearable. The second flashback: when parting and plaits are horribly crooked, my head looks crushed, my face distorted. That means my father was dead drunk the night before – my mother was crying as she combed my hair, I was a nuisance, a burden that, as she often said, made her shy away from divorce. And the third flashback: when both parting and plaits were straight, and the right and left sides of my face were symmetrical. That means my father came home sober the night before, my mother was elated, she managed to like me, she felt well. But the photos with the third flashback are rare. Photographers only came to the village on holidays. On weekdays my father drank during working hours. But on his days off, his only pastime was hitting the bottle. He had no time for the sort of games with which men used to while away their free time, no chess – or cards, no skittles, he didn't like dancing. He just sat there and drank till his eyes and his tongue bulged and his knees buckled. So my father's states are also documented in these photographic flashbacks. He had only three, and the following day they crept into my hair through the teeth of the comb.

Perhaps my mother's state of mind reached into my hair so visibly because she was deported to the Soviet Union for forced labour a few years before the time when she combed my hair. She spent five years in the camp as a guest of the king, who kills, and she was constantly starving during those five years. She was nineteen when she arrived at the camp, and like all peasant girls she had long plaits. She said reasons for shaving the head varied. There were two reasons and one always applied to her. Sometimes it was head lice, and sometimes, to avoid starving, she had stolen a few potatoes or beets from the field. Sometimes she was already shaven because of the lice and was also caught stealing. The guards regretted that you couldn't shave a head twice, the way you can thrash a back that has already been thrashed. Shaved stays shaved for a long time, she said to me. Hair is not as dumb as skin. There is a photograph of my mother as a shaven-headed girl, so emaciated the skin is sticking to the bones. She is holding a cat in her arms. The cat so skinny and its look so needle sharp, gaping, hungry eyes like my mother's. Every time I look at the photograph I ask myself: no matter how much she loved cats, why did an emaciated person share her meagre food with a cat. Was it to do with the hair the animal had and she didn't? The cat's coat is shaggy, the hair long and dishevelled, as if it had grown at the expense of the flesh into unnatural material that was alien to it.

And what about here in Germany? Why do Neo-Nazis shave their heads when they don't have to? They have a perverted relationship with themselves, no sense of self-abasement. They exploit their skulls, wear them disfigured like rocks, boulders in a shrunken or dried-up river bed. They are masquerading as a band of soldiers, turning self-hatred into a boast. In their brutalised world view they ennoble the perversion of the shaved head, freely adopt this stigma as a distinguishing mark of the group. Everything individual is erased in those boulder heads. Beneath the stitched bones of the shaved head lies a lamentable brain, controlled by the impulses of a member of the master race. Operating on instinct, the body becomes a tool for attack.

One of the first collages, in which I found rhyme and the king, goes like this:

In one hand
was the king sitting in the rain
that's how it was
to get away from myself
I went inside

in the other hand
the king was defeated
that's how it was
I went inside
and had my head shaved

There are two other important things that have to do with the king:

My grandfather's hair never fell out again. Thick and white, it went with him to his coffin.

Despite all the trouble my grandfather took with me, I never learned to play chess. He didn't think I had the brains for it, and I left it at that. I never told him how much I both feared and liked the king. My thoughts were not free, one might say.

Hunger and Silk

The Everyday Lives of Men and Women

The pickaxe threw off sparks. The salesman was hacking at the frozen red-blue stone. A queue stood before the scales. People with glassy eyes. They said little, as if the blows of the pickaxe made the tongue heavy. The point of the pickaxe kept breaking off chunks from the edge of the stone, some large, some small. Those who had moved to the front of the queue had curiosity written on their faces. And the question: How long will the stone last? Not long enough for everyone. Certainly not for those who are waiting in a queue three houses down the street.

The stone was made of chicken necks, wings, feet, heads. They had been laid in water and frozen.

Then the people at the head of the queue with their blue-red chunks went past those waiting, and headed home. On this day they had bought meat, they said. The sun shone down on cracked asphalt, half dead trees threw shadows composed only of branches. Those on the pavement were crooked antlers. A woman in high-heeled shoes walked past. For a few steps she carried the crooked antlers of the branches. And she carried the chunk next to the pale red silk dress.

A chicken's head – I could see it clearly next to the woman's thumb – watched her shoes as she walked. In the sun, the red-blue ice dripped next to her steps. A trail of drips where the woman had passed.

Hunger and silk, I thought. In the head was rage and helplessness. Those following walked with their chunks past the trail of drips in their shabby clothes. They doubled, tripled it. Soon the entire pavement was covered in trails of drips. They dried quickly, as if the hot asphalt wanted to hide what was going on here. Otherwise how would the street have looked: red-blue drips, like rain. Children, too, walked past, carrying the chunks in both hands. The drips seeped into their clothes.

Sometimes poverty announced itself only as poverty. It enclosed the faces, a look in the eyes like absence. The eyes like empty corridors, where the faces ran out. I could endure that, the same empty corridors looked and stretched from my eyes, no doubt. This poverty was not just hunger in the stomach. It was hunger as attitude to life. Hunger for sentences and gestures, for speaking. Hunger for laughter. Hunger for the noise that life makes.

Unbearable, impossible to endure with either the eyes or the skull, poverty was there displaying images, like those with the frozen stone of flesh. In those images the gulf opened up, through which flashed in a single moment all the misery of all who lived in this country, and the lack of dignity of all the years, all the lives. Or many moments like these.

Where hunger and silk met the image rolled over, became more than what you could see. The hunger in hunger turned on itself. You no longer knew what to do with yourself. It was too overwhelming. Impossible to look. Impossible to go there. Nor was it possible to go past, to make way. Twenty metres of asphalt enclosed the entire city. The entire country. The only place to hide from yourself was in your own head, until you were no longer aware of yourself, no longer knew who you were or where you were. You had to turn lifeless, not cry, not laugh, not scream. Not throw up. You could not fail to see that each person who followed a trail of drips counted for nothing. Nor did the others. Oneself included. You could not fail to see that only the dictator counted, 'the most beloved son of the people', he and his kin. You could not fail to see that every time this handful of rulers crooked a finger they did something that could not be grasped. Or grasped only in the images of hunger and silk.

Hunger and silk, the naked image of hunger. Not visible to the naked eye was what had been destroyed in people.

What could be seen: the regime does not allow its people to live. The regime keeps its people just alive, so as not to pay for burials.

Another overpowering image was the stuff of everyday life: coffins strapped to the roofs of cars, driving through the streets of the city, the names and ages of the dead written on them in large letters. They drove to the hospital. Or they came from the hospital. You saw these coffins and you knew there were bodies inside. Or there would soon be bodies inside.

The transport of the dead was left to families. The state didn't worry about it. Hospitals didn't accept elderly people. When you ordered an ambulance, the first question the doctor asked was: how old is the patient? If the invalid was over sixty-five, the emergency doctor didn't turn up.

Cars with coffins going down country roads were a common enough sight from the windows of a train. In the early morning or in the noonday heat the windows gleamed with green foliage, blooming grasses and endless fields of sunflowers or corn. The sunflowers had turned their heads. They looked towards the coffin, or they followed it. And in the winter the muck on the bare fields was a portent of the damp grave for the coffin on the car.

What could you think of when your hands trembled? Your own and those of others. This image too was overwhelming, you didn't know what to do with yourself: impossible to look, impossible to look away. Only one thought in the head: death. It affected everyone. Even the 'beloved son of the people'. And there was the question, how many people will Ceaușescu outlive? How long can he deal in the deaths of others before death strikes him down?

At those moments, you couldn't fail to see that the deaths of old people were a means of saving for the state. Death saved the state frozen chunks of meat and pensions.

The hospitals were swarming with cockroaches. They crawled up stairs, up the legs of the beds. They were the same flat, reddish beetles you saw behind the grocery store counters. The same creatures that crawled out in their hundreds, stunned by the heat, whenever I turned on the oven.

Every block of flats swarmed with these beetles. People referred to them, who knows why, as 'Russians'. I often found dead, dried out beetles pressed between pages when I took a book from the shelf.

'The cockroaches will outlive this nation,' a friend said, 'the cockroaches, the crows and the rats.'

In front of every block of flats the rubbish bins overflowed. In the summer they stank of rot. Rats ran around. Hungry, emaciated cats dragged food out of the rubbish bins. They mated on the rubbish bins in the middle of the day, between hungers. Howled. Sometimes children gathered to watch. Laughed. Grown-ups on their way past tried to separate the cats with stones and sticks.

These images too, swarming cockroaches, black clumps of crows that came into town from the fields, rats roaming around, skinny cats – these images too were stronger than reason. They tore one's eyes wide open and pressed them shut.

It was as if everything that moved, everything that lived in this country had to do with hunger. As if everything that lived had to reach the extreme, lurch, in order to live.

As if hunger were always intent on the crassest image of itself. On the crazed joke of hunger and silk.

The narrow margin of things one could call 'beautiful', which cropped up unexpectedly, was so close to wretchedness it no longer had any effect. Or it worked by way of contrast, such a tiny contrast that wretchedness, ugliness everywhere became even more pronounced.

When old peasant women stood on the street corners with wicker baskets selling little sparse bunches of snowdrops, lily of the valley, of garish summer flowers or autumn crocuses, the flowers made the faces of passers-by crumple. Because the flowers were so beautiful, because they had not lost the shimmer of the countryside, of the woods and river valleys and meadows, they made people sad. They belonged to the countryside. And 'countryside' was always the opposite of 'city'. They bloomed every year, to grow they required nothing. This doggedness of beauty so close to poverty sometimes seemed to me like indifference, like callousness towards human beings. In a state where survival has become the meaning of life, the beauty of the countryside becomes painful.

Flowers that contained the shimmer of the countryside were out of the question for state celebrations. At official occasions the most vacuous flowers were on display, red carnations. Red carnations, stiff and without scent, accompanied the hymns of praise to the dictator couple, school and office parties, conference rooms, concert stages, coffins of dead functionaries, driven through the city framed by red bunting and medals on slow-moving open-topped lorries.

The red carnation had long since abandoned the countryside and moved into the city. The red carnation was the flower of the powerful, the state flower, expressionless and durable. It had the obstinacy and ruthlessness of the powerful. It suited the celebration of power. The powerful liked it because it lacked the shimmer of the countryside, the quick withering, because it rustled instead of smelling.

Cedar, too, and silver fir, those unchanging, tall trees that bordered the villas of the *Nomenklatura* and guarded the shadowy secret behind pine needles that never fell, they too belonged among the flora of the powerful. They stood before institutions throughout the country. They were reliable, never turned yellow or bare. They didn't bloom. They didn't make the dignitaries feel insecure. Only when people in shabby clothes walked past them was there a contrast. Then they were in charge, they listened and watched. They grew on behalf of the powerful. They grew when I walked past them, against me and against all those in this country who had ever walked the streets with frozen chunks of meat.

The powerful had a sixth sense for plants and expressionless objects. Because they lacked expression they lent themselves to the adornment of power. They were suited to it. They were to be found again and again in places where people were degraded. This repetition, the persistence with which they accompanied power and everything to do with power, made red carnations, cedar and silver fir repulsive.

When it came to power and to hunger, repetition was the regime's most dependable method. It invariably made the powerful feel safe right away, and the powerless feel insecure right away.

The worse the situation in the country became, the more widespread was the repetition of ever diminishing objects.

The shops, the large 'Universal Shops' throughout the country, were filled with a few of the same things. In the grocery stores the shelves contained two kinds of tin can and two kinds of preserving jar. There were cans of fish and jars of jam, both inedible. They were part of the shop's fixtures and fittings. They had lingered for years on the same shelf, filthy, the labels yellowed and warped. Whether you travelled through the north or south of the country, the east or west, in summer or in winter, there they were, the tin cans in every grocery store.

It was no different in the clothes shops, floors of dresses made from the same material, in the same patterns, of the same colours. Up and down the country. The same heavy, stifling smell lay over every shop, generated by the impregnating agents used on the materials. Even in dazzling sunlight, the shops were in half darkness, for the colours of the clothes were dark. Not grey, but dusty grey. Not brown, but dusty brown. People went from rack to rack through many square metres of the dusty repetition. Sometimes when I went into a clothes shop I thought of the priest's pronouncement at burials: from dust we were created and to dust we shall return. Written all over the faces of the shop assistants.

The clothes did the opposite of clothing people. They covered them. They were sewn to make everyone who wore them seem grey on grey. In the shop they looked like columns, marching silently in step. With their colours, their shapelessness and the heavy, stifling smell of the impregnating agents, they looked like uniforms. They were meant to make people disappear under other people. For the powerful did not wear these clothes. They wore clothes from the West, or tailor-made suits.

The clothes that looked like columns of uniforms in the shop were worn only by those who queued for the frozen chunks of meat.

Every time I was in the clothes shops I could see in the half darkness and in the stifling air how little the individual counted in this country. Every time I was in a shop I thought: if they were now to say to me, take something you like, take everything you like, it's a gift from us to you, I would leave the shop empty-handed. I was often afraid they might make such an offer. I often felt obliged to decide on something, to declare my loyalty to a single piece of clothing. To introduce me to myself in this garment. Then the whole shop became a hunt. I left swiftly, in flight from ugliness.

That they were dependent on these clothes made people small and immature. That they paid money for them, a lot of money, for which they had worked many hours. That when they had bought these clothes, the circle closed: as they walked through the streets in these clothes you could tell they had to stand in queues for the frozen chunks of meat. That they belonged to those who counted for nothing in this country. They turned their heads longingly to follow those who walked past them in Western clothing. Desire sparkled in their eyes, through the empty corridors that hung in their gazes and down their wretched grey clothes.

Longing drove the people in the column clothing to buy the trivia of the powerful, things they took for granted, for a lot of money and for special occasions. Sometimes a pack of foreign cigarettes, a foreign cigarette lighter, a gleaming ballpoint pen would peer, consciously displayed, from the jacket or shirt pocket of a piece of column clothing.

The longing often went so far that the people in their column clothing put Rumanian cigarettes in Western cigarette packs to create the impression that the objects the powerful took for granted were within their grasp.

If the people in the column clothing had bought foreign cigarettes for a lot of money, they only smoked them in public. Cigarettes, lighters, pens were status symbols. They attracted attention, admiration. They saw to it that people in column clothing achieved recognition. Naturally, recognition from their own kind.

Packaging for Western goods was used as decoration in people's apartments. Or on desks in offices. Empty Coke cans, beer cans, coffee cans, little perfume bottles. For the most part this packaging was not emptied by the people it sat in front of. It had been acquired empty, as a way of brushing up against the things the powerful took for granted. They were given empty to their owners. Sometimes they were even bought empty by their owners. In the flea markets empty Western packaging was offered for sale.

Plastic bags too, brightly coloured, foreign plastic bags attracted attention out on the streets. They were sold in the flea markets. The people in the column clothing carried them around, treated them carefully so they lasted. They didn't want them to get crumpled or dirty. They shone above the shattered, cracked asphalt.

When there were no trails of drips from the frozen chunks of meat, spit gleamed. Spitting on the pavement went with walking, men mostly. While out walking, one had to be careful not to step in the spit. This spit frequently consisted of green clumps of slime. Spitting had nothing to do with colds. It was a habit. It went with walking through the streets, was as normal as column clothes, dust or puddles. People made no attempt to disguise their spitting on the pavement. No one objected to it. No one was disgusted by the green clumps. They lay too in station waiting rooms, on platforms, on paths winding through the parks, in underpasses, under bridges, in the courtyards and corridors of companies. There were days when these green clumps irritated me. There were days when I didn't see them, because I was used to them. There were days when I liked these green clumps of spit. They were part of the city's descent into misery. Who could be repulsed by spit on the pavements of a country in which red-blue frozen chicken's heads and feet were eaten as meat. In which cockroaches traversed grocery stores and rats raced from one rubbish bin to another between apartment blocks. Repulsion no longer existed. And if it did exist it was a constant and one no longer felt it. For one lived in a world that was intent on shoving together everything that was ugly into the smallest possible space in dense, mindless repetition. Perfectly normal slices of reality had rips like collages. They pointed beyond themselves, they brushed against the crazed joke of hunger and silk.

People gave themselves over to their bodies. They did what their bodies asked. Like spitting, the men's gait was accompanied by ball scratching. The eye had become accustomed to this gesture, which was often long drawn out and conspicuous. It was so normal that it formed a part of men's conduct. Just as the word *pula*, meaning 'prick' was used thousands of times in all circumstances, in all conversations. 'What, my prick' sounded like 'what the hell'. Every minor irritation gave vent to the word *pula*. The word is not vulgar in Rumanian. The word 'cunt' was used just as often in various combinations.

The prudishness of the dictatorship ran counter to the people's natural use of this repertoire of words. In Rumanian when people are angry they say get fucked in the ear, the nose, the head. I have always envied this language for its vitality. Even now when I curse I speak Rumanian, because German has no curses so picturesque. The words are all there in German, but they aren't up to the job. They weigh heavy and are obscene.

At a company meeting a woman said in a rage: 'What the devil, my prick, do you want?' After the woman had calmed down she apologised for the word 'devil'. The people in the room laughed. Then the woman asked, offended: 'Why, my cunt, are you laughing?'

These words and phrases don't appear in the dictionary of the Rumanian language. In the official media and for the censors they belonged in the drawer marked pornography. They were banned. In everyday life these words and phrases were the only lightness for the people with the empty corridors in their gazes. I think they helped them survive, endure the crazed joke of hunger and silk.

When someone interfered in matters that didn't concern them the Rumanians said: 'Sorrow fucks you.' This was both malevolent and good-natured. You would have to string a lot of sentences together in German to express the same thing. And because it would involve so many sentences what was contained in this one would be lost. I've often tried to translate expressions from Rumanian into German. To use them in German. Then I felt deprived of all the nuance of my mother tongue.

Every time I heard these words and phrases in snatches of conversation on the street I knew the regime had driven this lively population into suspended animation. Into numbness.

And sometimes I thought this language absorbed all anger, because it was so colourful. That protest, with all of the long, angry curses, lodged in the sentences.

To this day, when I speak with a Rumanian friend in exile, these words and expressions come straight into the conversation, into the sentences. And my friend says, 'Say that again. It's so long since I've heard it.' He says it as a joke, and it is meant seriously. And I repeat the words and expressions as a joke, and mean them seriously.

The representatives of the regime avoided this language. I often asked myself whether they fell back on it among themselves. The empty phrases and prefabricated components of their ideology, which had taken so much from this language, had become so numerous over twenty years that they were enough. You could open and shut your mouth for hours, talk without saying anything. Through the cult of the personality Ceauşescu and his wife were the only rulers in the country. All the other powerful people were vassals. They had to represent the power of the ruling couple, they had to invoke the ruling couple in everything they said. They had to re-chew the language of the ruling couple. That's why their language was the ultimate vassal language. Just as the people who had empty corridors in their gaze and column clothing on their backs wanted to touch the certainties of the powerful through foreign cigarette packs and lighters and ballpoint pens, so they also appropriated their language, often without realising it.

Two months after the revolution the writer Mircea Dinescu said in a *Spiegel* interview: 'After forty years of no free newspapers the ways of speaking and thinking don't change in the course of a few weeks. If you give a television set from which the word "cuckoo" chimes constantly to a native tribe the natives will learn to say nothing except "cuckoo".'

The representatives of power, those who spoke most clearly the language of the vassal, had different faces. Their cheekbones ground as they spread their dead language across the country. No empty corridors in their eyes when they re-chewed the dictator's prefabricated parts. They never had an ideal yet they always had a goal, to preserve their power with every means available, to distinguish themselves through privileges from those who stood in a queue before the frozen stone of meat.

The language of the vassal opened a yawning gulf in the face of the wretchedness in the country. The language of the vassal was lies and derision down to the last breath, devised to be parroted by everyone. It promoted no ideal, only self-contempt and blind repetition, until one's own thinking was numbed, shrunken and forgotten. Or merely turned senseless circles in the head, without a voice, without its own voice. The language of the vassal transformed one's own thought into a kind of bad conscience.

Bad conscience made people so small they shrank to the value the regime placed on them. Life itself, drawing breath, had a whiff of the forbidden. This prohibition, like fear, was everywhere. It didn't need to be spelled out.

Fear fantasies sprang up. They circulated like whispered fairy tales: Ceaușescu was seriously ill. He would be long dead if not for daily blood transfusions, the blood extracted with a needle from the foreheads of newborn babies. Women whispered these spine-chilling tales to each other in faltering voices. They were being reduced to birthing machines. Prophylactics were banned. The pill was banned. Women were only permitted to have abortions if they had had five children or were older than forty-five. Women's wombs were watched over through compulsory examinations at regular intervals.

I heard the whispered fairy tale about the dictator's blood transfusions from a woman graduate no older than thirty who lived in the city. I was doubtful about the story. She was not.

A few days later a colleague, a teacher at the same school, told me on the way home she had a problem. She was pregnant. 'You don't have children. You must know a doctor who can help,' she said.

I told her I didn't. I said I'd never been pregnant. I lied. I didn't know my colleague that well. I was afraid everything she was saying was a provocation. Only when she started trembling and crying did I believe her.

She sensed that I believed her. She calmed down and I felt guilty. She looked at me with the empty corridors in her eyes. I stared at the ground. She said softly, yet fiercely, 'I've told my husband I'll cut off his prick if it happens again.'

The woman had two children.

After sitting in the park on a bench made up of two narrow boards and missing a backrest, I said, 'I'm on the pill. I've done two abortions myself – myself, you understand?' She nodded.

What I had said was in keeping with the truth.

A few weeks later the pregnant teacher was on a stage in the town youth centre. There was yet another competition between schools for the 'Glory to Rumania' festival. I could only see my pregnant colleague from behind. She was conducting a choir in a hymn of praise to Ceauşescu. How can she stand it? I asked myself.

Then the summer holidays began. The following year I was working at a different school. I often thought of the pregnant woman. I met her by chance one day in the city. I came up to her laughing, for she should have been in her sixth month, and she wasn't. Her stomach was flat. 'I'm glad you've solved the problem you had back then.' I said. She looked me briefly in the eye. Her look was cold. 'I don't know what you're talking about,' she said. I left.

There was a family counselling centre in the district hospital. The doctor responsible for counselling was married to a secret service officer. Trusting in her meant trusting in the secret service.

A medical student in her final year was pregnant. She performed an abortion on herself. In the days that followed she developed a high fever. She should have gone to hospital. Out of fear of the hospital and out of fear of a prison sentence she hanged herself in a room in a student hostel. After the funeral at a meeting of the university management and in the presence of other students she was excluded post mortem from the party and expelled from the university. A photo of her was hung in the hall of the student hostel where she had hanged herself. It was accompanied by a few words portraying the dead woman as a 'negative example'.

'Doctors' from the secret service were employed at the women's clinics. Specialists in interrogation, they were disguised as doctors, wore white coats and 'Dr' preceded their names. After they were taken to hospital, women were interrogated about the abortion procedure. The people who had supplied the means or were accessories had to be denounced. Treatment was initiated only after the information had been surrendered, even when there was a haemorrhage. Women often died because they would not confess.

In the course of a working day female workers were frequently brought for examination to the gynaecologist, escorted by a 'trustworthy' company person. The explanation was 'prevention of cancer of the womb'. Yet these 'preventative' examinations didn't exist before the abortion laws were tightened. Pregnant women were registered. Besides, any medical treatment on a woman was only undertaken after the woman had presented a certificate from the gynaecologist, a certificate required even for a dental appointment.

At a meeting of the school management it was decided to expel a schoolgirl because she was pregnant. The suggestion was made by the class teacher. The pregnant schoolgirl was not allowed to attend the meeting. The outcome of the meeting was clear before the meeting even began. The men and women who spoke were following instructions. Even the order in which they spoke was pre-determined. An 'insider' took the minutes. Unexpected remarks would not have been recorded in the minutes of the meeting. I spoke up, said that we

were a school, that we had to be there for a girl who had problems.
What was to become of her? I asked. She would end up on the
street. I said that sex education was missing from the curriculum. I
said too that the man, whose child the schoolgirl was expecting,
wanted nothing to do either with her or the child. And that the
parents had thrown their pregnant daughter out of the house because
of the 'shame'. My comments aroused the anger of the school
management (two women). The appointed speakers and the minute-
taker felt personally attacked. But most of those present gave me a
bored look and kept quiet. Then a vote was taken, all in favour,
except my own. 'That's outrageous,' said the class teacher, 'we're a
school, a secondary school, not a welfare institution.' During breaks
the pregnant schoolgirl was taunted and jeered in the corridor by the
other pupils. Those who didn't taunt and jeer avoided her and said
nothing.

This school story took place in 1984. Two years later the dictator's orders had changed, as had the procedure. The class teachers
were given the task of telling the schoolgirls what a great honour it
was to become a mother. In the event of a pregnancy schoolgirls
could continue the school year straight after the birth of the child.
They could hand the child over to the orphanages. For ever, too.
After the fall of Ceaușescu it was discovered that orphan children
were sold to the West for hard currency. And that the special forces
among the secret services came from the orphanages.

The mother of a schoolgirl in the sixth class came to school and told the class teacher that her husband, the girl's father, had been sexually abusing her daughter for half a year. The mother had learned of it from the younger daughter. She had left work early the day before to be sure. She had found her husband in bed with the elder daughter. The daughter had said nothing to her mother because of the father's threats. The mother found the daughter as guilty as the husband. The class teacher and the school management approved of this guilty verdict. A week later the schoolgirl was shipped to a school for children with learning difficulties.

I was working in a mechanical engineering factory. At a desk next to mine in the office I overheard a phone conversation: 'Hello. Do you still sell hand embroidery? The size is twenty-nine by two. How much will that be? Good. When can I collect the embroidery? Yes, I'll be there at ten a.m.' A colleague of mine was talking. She had a child. She was twenty-nine years old and in the second month of her pregnancy – those were the measurements of the embroidery. She was talking to a back-street abortionist. The cost of the abortion was 5,000 Lei (two months' wages). My colleague was lucky. The abortion was carried out with no complications. When she was pregnant again six months later she performed the abortion herself with the plastic tube of a circular knitting needle. One year later she inserted this tube into my womb in the factory toilet. I wore the tube for three days and three nights. The free end was stuck to my thigh. I had to go about in dresses to ensure the passage of air into the womb. With a second abortion I did it alone. My office colleague lent me her plastic tube. Behind the locked door of my flat I crouched in the bathroom over a mirror I had placed on the floor. I inserted the tube into my womb.

An acquaintance said, 'No problem. When my wife is pregnant we drive for the weekend to my mother-in-law's in the country. Lift up the cellar door twenty times, done. You just have to find a way.' I didn't know his wife well. I asked myself if she could say that so casually.

Recipes for abortions circulated like the whispered fairy tales about Ceauşescu's state of health:

Insert finely ground curd soap into the womb
Insert lemon juice or citric acid into the womb
Insert the plastic tube of a circular knitting needle into the
    womb
Lift heavy furniture as often, as high and for as long as
    possible
Take an overdose of various injections, twice, three days apart
Take an overdose of the stomach tablets that were smuggled
    into the country from the Soviet Union and sold on the
    black market: over twenty-four hours, two tablets every
    two hours. Fever, stomach cramps and heavy vomiting
    were supposed to bring about the abortion. The tablets
    were known as 'Russian Bonbons'.

These recipes were not just whispered. They were also applied. People began with the more harmless versions and moved with increasing desperation to the hazardous ones. Day after day such abortion methods led in hundreds of cases to death. Today nobody knows how many women have died as a result of the abortion law. How many died alone at home, how many in hospital under the eyes of the specialist interrogators. No statistics were kept. Just as prophylactics and the pill were banned, so too were statistics. The dead women were entered into the statistics with falsified diagnoses. Doctors who had recorded a particularly high number of births could look forward to prizes and rapid career advancement.

A female student was arrested with five fellow students.

All six of them were travelling to a village close to the Yugoslav border. The parents of one of the students lived in this village. The grounds for arrest were invented: 'attempted, illegal border crossing'. Not one of the six people had left the car and the car had not left the road. As writers, the five fellow students were already known to the secret service for their 'subversive activities'. During the interrogation that followed they were locked in neighbouring cells. The female student ended up in another wing of the prison, in a large communal cell with prostitutes. During the interrogation the policeman grabbed her breast and her behind. She defended herself. The policeman said in a rage, 'Don't be a hypocrite. How many kilometres of prick have you sucked on in your life.' He threatened to beat her. Fearful of torture, she gave in. He pretended he wanted to kiss her. She closed her eyes and decided to endure it. As his face approached hers he slapped her twice, scornfully. Afterwards he claimed she had tried to seduce him. The student was brought back weeping to the cell. The women in the cell greeted her with laughter. 'You're a softie. But you'll get over it. You're here because of the pricks, just like us.'

Having children was women's work in Rumania. Men were mostly of the opinion that women had to deal with what's inside them. They said, with the confidence with which they scratched their balls as they walked, 'Women have to be beaten, can't happen often enough. If the man doesn't know why, then the woman certainly does.'

The wives and daughters of the *Nomenklatura* were not affected by the tougher abortion laws. They had their state within a state, abortions took place in the party hospitals. Only women who queued in shops for frozen chunks of meat had five children. They had neither the contacts nor the money for an abortion. Theirs were the children of poverty, with eyes far too deep and empty corridors, even as they learned to walk and talk. Who, even as children, had to go places where hunger and silk brushed against each other. They were children neither the mother nor the father had wished for. Nothing more than the lesser evil, the alternative to prison or death.

The question kept arising: why did Ceauşescu want this population growth, more and more people in a country lacking in basic foods. 'Comrade Nicolae Ceauşescu is the father of all children, and comrade Elena Ceauşescu is the mother of all children,' children heard from Kindergarten. They had to repeat it to cripple their own thoughts. And the most horrifying thing of all is that, in a macabre way, it was true for many of them.

I fear that one day many children will discover why they exist. People will talk about the dictatorship, will have to talk: in the media, in schools, at home. The third, fourth, fifth child of a mother will not be able to overlook the connection between the pressure on a woman to give birth and their own life. Even though Ceauşescu is long dead there will again be empty corridors in many eyes. A fact no one can alter will hang over many lives, even if this law was rescinded immediately after Ceauşescu's death.

Just as, following a war, the word 'war' is still there, must still be there, in the phrase 'post war', so too in the time after Ceauşescu the name Ceauşescu will still, must still, be there for a long time to come. Like other dictators throughout history, Ceauşescu achieved the immortality he strived for, in reverse. He died but did not vanish. His fingerprints are all over the country as ruined cities and villages, as ravaged landscape, as the trail of blood of those who were shot when he fell, as terror beneath the skull of the survivors. Ceauşescu's dreams are cemeteries across the country.

And every bit as great as the terror, which continued daily, is the terror of past terror. Everyone who lives or has lived in Rumania, everyone who has survived Ceauşescu, has outlived him by only a short time. Each survivor is marked. With the terror beneath his skull he will have to reflect on past terror to reach an understanding. To understand himself. Each of their lives will break into two parts, the time before Ceauşescu and the time after.

And wherever hunger and silk have brushed against each other once, then again and again, where out of lunacy a whole country, crowded into a few square metres, rolled over in front of your eyes, there is fear. Obstinate and tough, as rhythmic as a second heartbeat in the knees, it accompanies your steps.

A few days ago a man asked me if I thought it possible that, instead of Ceauşescu, one of his doubles was executed. The man had never lived in Rumania, he had visited the country after the fall of Ceauşescu. The man asked the question in the tone of whispered fairy tales. 'I don't think so,' I replied. 'Ceauşescu no longer exists,' I said. 'I heard his voice at the trial. And I saw his gestures. And those of his wife. That was no double.'

The man had brought the fear in his face from Rumania. The fingerprints of the dead dictator only become visible in the bleakness and aimlessness of the new freedom. They are the echo of the scream. The wretchedness of the country can't be cleared away from one day to the next. Poverty is apparent through angry gestures and voices, now grown loud. The empty corridors are still there, in people's gazes, visible to everyone, even a foreigner. The rumours of terror and the whispers will be there for a long time. Everyone will hear them and pass them on, even a foreigner. They create emotions.

They provide a possibility for the inhabitants and the foreigners to participate in what is happening, not thinking politically.

The man who had visited Rumania would rather have heard me say something other than what I did say. When I answered him his face didn't change. As he left, he carried the fear in his face away from me. And incredulity. After he had taken a few steps he looked round. He even stood still mid-step before he noticed that he had to take this answer away with him. Not even at that moment would it have been too late for him to hear the opposite of what I'd said. I hadn't reassured him with my answer. I had upset him.

If I'd said I think it's possible that not Ceaușescu but one of his doubles was executed, the man and I would have had a long conversation. As he addressed me the man was ready for that. His expectations had not been met and he made off as if my answer had driven him away.

Such a Big Body
and Such a Small Engine

So many photos hanging on the walls, you could no longer see the wall. In one photo Father was the bridegroom. You could see only half his chest. The other half was a bouquet of tattered white flowers Mother held in her hand. Their heads were so close together their earlobes were touching. In another photo Father stood bolt upright in front of a fence. Snow lay under his boots. The snow so white Father stood in empty space. His hand raised above his head in greeting. Runes on the collar of his coat. In the next photo Father was sitting at the wheel of a lorry. The lorry was laden with cattle. Every week Father drove the cattle to the slaughterhouse in town.[16]

Lived experience vanishes into time and resurfaces in literature. I've never written about lived experience one to one, but only in roundabout ways. And I've always had to make sure that what is unreal and invented can represent what is real and actually happened.

I started to write after the death of my father. Not after his actual death, but after being at his side through a chronologically short but in my experience endlessly long illness, for it was without hope or mercy. And when it had eaten up the body, when the head was as small as a bird's and the nose as big as a beak and the neck as thin as a candle – it was still the same person lying there in bed, but at the same time he was no more than an object, what was alive had departed the body. It fluttered outside in the February air. When I left him lying in the hospital just after he'd died, ragged, handkerchief-sized scraps of snow began to fall, for these were no flakes. The falling snow disgusted me, made me feel dizzy, I looked only at the ground, watched my shoes as I walked and yet I walked without feet, as if my eyes were wearing shoes. In the fluttering snow I understood that this day of death was hurling around the scraps of my childhood. Admittedly it was terrifying, but it was unequivocal rather than supernatural. You could look at it soberly: the weather allowed itself this extravagance. And something new began when my father's life came to an end – a few days later I began to write, although I had no such plans nor anything to do with literature in mind. And since that was how writing had threaded its way into my life I wrote about my father from the start, and then again and again. For while he was alive his life constantly mirrored mine.

That was because I knew I must love him, although I couldn't – and at the same time I knew I loved him, though I didn't want to. This insoluble problem had to do with the *Oberscharführer*, with the Waffen SS. Most of the German minority in the Banat and in Siebenburgen too were passionate about Hitler. The same applies to my father, who at the time was not yet my father. In 1943 he volunteered with all of his seventeen years for the Waffen SS. He was probably a 'capable' soldier, he reached the rank of *Oberscharführer*. That was all he would speak of. The war itself was not mentioned in a single sentence. As far as he was concerned the war ended right after he enlisted. He didn't have his blood group tattooed on his arm, he was able to throw away his SS uniform and pass for a soldier in the German army and was held in an English POW camp. Twenty years later he told us the story with roguish pride. That was all that needed to be known. In the seventies he still sang Nazi songs in the village with his comrades from the war, but it was risky asking him about the war, he was an alcoholic and prone to outbursts of rage.

So a lorry driver and an alcoholic. A good combination. He was compulsive, forever in search of risk. It was a spirited search, allied to an irritable tongue and coarse wit. He needed danger and excess. When I was making my way from the hospital into town, utterly at a loss with death in my head and the white handkerchief scraps of snow around me, this came into my head: my father is seated in front of me on a chair, his torso sways as he sits, as if on water. He is drunk, blind drunk, unable to put his shoes on. But he says, we have to get out of here before night falls. And I kneel down on the ground and shove his feet into his shoes and tie the laces. He stands up, staggers over to the lorry and climbs in. I sit down beside him and we set off. We are up in the mountains, driving along narrow winding roads, half in the clouds. On the mountain side cliffs reach up to the sky, on the valley side cliffs reach down to the abyss. This journey lasts at least five hours, until the road leads from sky to earth, where the plains begin and you can no longer plunge down.

We drove this road out of the mountains four or five times a year. Every few weeks throughout the summer he drove vegetables to the mountains for the agricultural cooperative. Two or three days later, after everything had sold out, we drove back. I felt no fear when he was driving drunk round hairpin bends. That's how it had to be, because that's how he was. He was my father, I was his child, and I trusted him. I thought, if something happens then the dark forest and the white Steingebirge will punish us. If misfortune befalls us the region is guilty and not he. Nothing ever happened. Occasionally someone stood waving on a deserted road, a man or woman with a heavy rucksack or basket on their back who wanted to ride on the empty trailer to the next or the next-but-one far-flung mountain or place. But when the lorry stopped and my father got out to negotiate the price and open the tailgate to let them up, these strangers smelled his breath, heard him slurring his words, watched him staggering. They shook their heads and preferred to go on foot. What fools, I thought, nothing would happen to them, this region won't punish them, they are at home here in this precipitous landscape.

'He can only drive away from himself,' said my grandfather, he also meant all that drinking. One time his lorry was in the yard at home, it had broken down. My father was repairing it. The neighbour walked round it and said, 'Such a big body and such a small engine.'

A sentence like that says a lot, sticks in your head right away because it sounds so naïvely melancholy and so innocently comic at the same time, and because its duplicity applies to so many things. A sentence like that is a parable in itself. In many situations it comes to you as a running commentary on what is happening and, for no apparent reason, it comes as a surprise. Not only do you realise that it works, but it encapsulates the entire event. The course of events adjusts itself promptly to the sentence. It's suddenly the high point of the event.

When my father was dead I kept picturing him in his lorry, having skidded into other drivers on the city streets, and I thought, 'Such a big body and such a small engine.' I wasn't referring to the lorry any more, but to death. And I saw the big body and the small engine when I watched the cockroaches on the shelves for half an hour or an hour while queuing for bread in the shop, how athletically and elegantly they crawled along, and by contrast the people – how hamstrung and timid they were as they silently showed the shopkeeper their identity card before receiving their bread. And I also thought of the big body and the small engine in the market when the melon salesman was shaving behind the mountain of melons, when he had no customers. I watched him scraping off the white foam with a folding knife while staring into a halved water melon, the mirror pressed deep into the red flesh of the melon so it wouldn't topple over. And when it struck me as unseemly that you wish someone luck in Rumanian by saying, May luck strike you dead. And when I marvelled that the shoe has a tongue, the apple a core, the shoulder a blade, the ear a drum, the knee a cap, the nail a head – when the contents of words obsessed me through the names of things, the audacity with which living beings and dead objects help each other, because things have qualities and we have eyes in our head which observe. Or when I listened for quite a while in the factory washroom and still couldn't tell whether the crane operator under the shower next to mine was singing or crying, and when I finally asked her and she said: both. And when I put on make-up, because I had been summoned to the secret service and had no idea when, how or if I would ever get out of there, or when the secret service locked me into the office in the factory and I had to pay attention for hours on end to what I said, and where it was better to remain silent, when my heart was beating so fast it almost leapt into my mouth, but my tongue became so heavy it almost fell through my mouth and down to the heart, when I could no longer see the sense of life, would gladly have been dead and thought about suicide but couldn't kill myself, because the interrogator was threatening to murder me and wanted me to die, and when, utterly weary and against all good sense, I clung to life out of defiance – not to carry out the regime's dirty work against me – in every one of these circumstances what came into my head again and again was the sentence: 'Such a big body and such a small engine.'

The sentence soothed me, because it startled in a laconic way. I don't know exactly what it means. And I don't want to know. And even if I wanted to, I couldn't. What I do know: there is no final sense or official status in this sentence, there is no sovereign meaning, no higher authority. Sometimes this sentence doesn't believe what it says. And most of the time it doesn't tell me what it believes: such big paraphernalia and so little truth. It seems to me this difference between things is always there.

My father's decision to volunteer for the Waffen SS when he was seventeen was a warning to me at the age of seventeen. I believe that at seventeen one has reached the age of reason, one is an adult. Many people already had jobs at this age, were married, even had children. In the course of a lifetime one grows up many times and always differently, but at seventeen one has grown up for the first time, if not for the second or fifth. At seventeen one has experienced the difference between good and evil thousands of times.

153

Every child knew that in public you never say what you think and you never do what you want. Outside your own front door life is divided in two: there is what you are not allowed to do because it is forbidden, and what you have to do because you are forced to. Every child sensed that this oppression was the prevailing mood and understood that we were living in a dictatorship, without ever having this explained to them in theory. The state of affairs was clear, no one had to use the word dictatorship. We didn't even know it. We knew the words party and police, they governed our fear. And we knew as children that both were evil and not good, you could feel it through the pores in your skin. And we knew too that there was advantage and disadvantage for political reasons. We needed no theoretical explanation of political reasons.

I once had to recite a party poem on stage at a school festival. For weeks I learned it by heart. But when it was time to go on stage I was overcome by fear that I would get stuck and bring shame on the school, the party, the village, maybe even the fatherland. The fear of this reproach erased the poem from my head. Trembling, I went on stage and twisted the bottom button of my jacket with my left hand. I braced myself, clung to the button and instead of uttering the title of the poem, 'The Party', I said 'The Swallow' in desperation. Suddenly it was as if I had climbed into someone else's skin, I kept twiddling the jacket button and flawlessly recited every verse of the swallow poem. Twiddling the button protected me, the fear reached a peak then retreated, I no longer felt I had to do anything and I changed the poem. The revolving jacket button worked like the wheel of an engine. By way of the jacket button I was using my head through my fingers. Such a big body and such a small engine in two senses: the turning of the button and of me. And also with regard to the glaring difference between the two poems: the party poem was such a vast, oppressive body, and the swallow poem was such a small, nimble engine. But after I had recited the poem the fear rose again, for I knew this had consequences. The season for swallows was all wrong – 30 December, the Day of the Republic. I was punished by the school authorities, two weeks of house arrest, in other words I couldn't leave the house for the whole winter holiday. And of course the neighbour found out, the same neighbour who said of my father's broken down lorry, '*such a big body and such a small engine*'. He was amused by my house arrest: 'You and your swallow, you might as well have said the swallow is flying out of the party.'

The swallow hurt the party – this was in the village. Several years later things got more serious. I moved to the city and the state was everywhere. And anyone who worked on people's fears in the service of the state could build a career. Now I was seventeen, as my father was back then, and the thought that he enlisted in the SS at my age was with me. I had to make up my mind to strive for nothing at secondary school, to come across as neither too clever nor too stupid, to swim in midstream but pay close attention. Steer clear, play dumb, remain cussed – this tactic worked for three to four years. Then, no longer. I was a student and at that age you no longer live according to the dictates of fate. You seek out people, friends with whom you have something in common. Your preferences are no longer secret, soon the state knows what's going on. My friends, the people of my own age I came to love, were already enemies of the state as students, caught in the cross hairs of the regime. And by associating with them I too became an enemy. That was fine by me and perfectly normal, for everything I liked most about these friends was strictly forbidden and severely punished by this state. And what I'd heard from my friends became clear: if you are an enemy, the state treats you in a loathsome manner. In the course of an interrogation the interrogator tried to turn me into a spy. I responded to his direct approach by being direct myself, 'That is not in my character,' I said to him. 'I don't want to become like you.'

This refusal had as its point of departure my father's joining in. First and foremost I didn't want to be like him at seventeen, because in all the years that followed you could tell from his behaviour that once you get entangled it never stops, that you constantly treat yourself and others badly, how coarse you must be when you've made mistakes and you know things about yourself no one else can know, when you strut around incorrigibly proud with a bad conscience. As a child I loved him very much. Later, I kept building the distance against that love. And it kept closing up, and I kept building it. In the meantime I knew from my own daily life of things shattered, of nerves like torn twine, of mortal fears that make your brain as rigid as a white stone in your head.

My father has been dead for thirty years, and I continue to worry about his life. Or should I say: over his life. And precisely because I know mortal fear for political reasons through my own baggage, I reproach him for belonging to the Waffen SS, for having hounded others into mortal fear. Why shouldn't I? This reproach is the least of it. He believed in Hitler, wanted Hitler to win the war, although he was a witness to those crimes. He is part of the Master from Germany that Celan portrayed in his 'Death Fugue'. I read books. I must place him in his own time and that of certain authors. He is one of those who brought fear to Jorge Semprún, Georges-Arthur Goldschmidt, Jean Améry, Aharon Appelfeld, Imre Kertész, Ruth Klüger, Louis Begley. To Primo Levi, Paul Celan and Walter Hasenclever. He did armed service, he wore the uniform that spelled death for those I have just named. What can I do but reproach him for it.

At seventeen I was extremely fearful, and I was still fearful at twenty-five, and at thirty perhaps even more so, because a lot had happened. No choice but to stay with my resolve: I will not do what others want me to do. In the midst of all that fear my one thought was: I don't want them to use burnt matchsticks for me.

The grandparents who lived at home were my mother's parents. In their bedroom above the bed hung the wedding photo of their son, my uncle Matz, whom I knew only from hearsay. There was also a startled-looking bride in the photograph. Above her veil a steep crown of wax flowers, not a braided garland but a hoop of scrawny white leaves that looked like twisted icicles. And the bride-groom with his stony face in his SS uniform. He had leave from the front to get married and went straight back to the war. And straight after the wedding his wife was a widow. It was the last photo of him.

He was 'a fervent believer', according to my mother. He was the son of the grain merchant, the rich man in the village. And he owed his wealth to a Jewish family, the Hirsches, who had advanced him a great deal of money as an interest-free loan when he started his firm. My grandparents' family were close friends with the Hirsch family, every summer they and their children came with us on holiday. Matz was a child at the time. And then, because his father grew wealthy, he went to a secondary school in the city. There were Nazi teachers from the Reich at the school. There he became a 'fervent believer', a Nazi and an anti-Semite. In the village, this godforsaken dump at the edge of the world, he considered himself to be the Führer's representative, climbed up on wine barrels and made speeches, hectored and preached at the young like some village ideologue, blackmailed and denounced. He was dogged, possessed. His father said at the time, 'He's under Hitler's spell.' Now, my mother says he was unrecognisable.

During the Stalinist era of the fifties a policeman could enter your house at any time for no reason, and it was risky to display a bridegroom in SS uniform in a picture frame. Perhaps because he wanted to change something about his son even after his death, or perhaps simply in anticipation of possible difficulties, or for both reasons, my grandfather painted over the runes on the photograph with spit and burnt matchsticks. He drank two glasses of schnapps before taking the photo from its frame. He had never been drunk in his life, but for this correction to his son he wanted to grant himself a bit of Dutch courage – or a bit of talent. He frequently painted the picture, every couple of weeks, maybe only to busy himself with his son. He could never get the colour of the uniform's collar quite right. It couldn't be done with soot from the match, not even when schnapps was added to the spit. This bridegroom remained forever in uniform, the filthy little runes squinting from the tips of the collar, never closing their eyes. Here too this sentence, this melancholy joke applies: 'Such a big body and such a small engine.'

When We Don't Speak We Become Unbearable –
When We Do We Make Fools of Ourselves

Keeping silent is not a pause while speaking, but something altogether different. From the peasants back home I became familiar with a way of life in which the use of words was not common practice. If you never speak about yourself you don't talk much. The more someone was able to keep silent, the stronger their presence. Like everyone in the house, I too had learned to interpret the twitch of a wrinkle, the jugular, nostril, corner of the mouth, the chin or the finger, and not wait for words to come. Among these silent people our eyes had learned what mood someone was dragging around the house. We listened with our eyes more than with our ears. An agreeable ponderousness, a long drawn out, heavy weight of things we carry in our heads. Words can't offer such heft, they don't stand still. Once spoken, as the last syllable sounds, they are mute. And they can only be spoken singly, one after another. Each sentence takes its turn only as the previous one has departed. With silence everything comes up at once, everything that has long remained unsaid, and what has never been said, stays hanging in the air. It's a stable, self-contained state. Speech is a thread that bites through itself and must be constantly reattached.

When I arrived in the city I was amazed at how much the city folk have to talk to be able to feel alive, to be friend or foe to each other, to give or to receive. And above all how much they complain when they talk about themselves. Most of their conversations were a constant pairing of arrogance and self-pity, the whole body given over to narcissistic posturing. Always running around with that worn 'I' in their mouths. Their theatricality was supple, the city folk had different joints beneath the skin, the tongue in their mouth the whole person. I, who had practised silence for so long and brought with me my heavy village bones, who at first spoke not a word of Rumanian, and later only haltingly, felt inhibited by this compulsion to speak. I attributed the constant replicating of the individual to the man-made surroundings under open skies. Streets, squares, river banks, parks – paving or asphalt everywhere, not only smoother than the village paths, but smoother than the floors of the best rooms inside the houses. More man-made it seemed to me than the summer kitchens in the village, which had clay floors. I needed an explanation and I grasped the simplest one: when one's feet are on a smooth surface, the tongue feels compelled to speak without thinking. The fields don't permit that, they are bumpy and set on decomposition. One responds to the asphalt with speech, to the fields with the heavy slowness of the bones, unprotected, one stretches out time, knowing the earth is greedy, one lets the tongue lie still in the mouth and the earth wait. On the asphalt one becomes lighter. By talking incessantly death is not below, but behind life. I was homesick and had a bad conscience, as if I had made off, leaving others to face the greedy village soil with its flourishing waxworks of the forms of death. I was used to seeing death as part of daily life. Death sought me out because I thought of it before the state came to me with its death threats. It sought me out where the covered earth in the city came to an end. It lurked in the fringes of the city, which were perhaps the fringes of my childhood, on the concrete tables of the vegetable market, where old women from the mountains sold nut-sized bitter peaches coated in grey down. Their faces resembled the skin, they were peach crones. Death lurked in the parks when the young, reddish leaves in the alleys of poplar trees smelled like the rooms of old people. And death sat pale as wax the length of the streets, in blooming lime trees when their yellow dust fell to earth. The lime trees smelled different on the asphalt, there were countless lime trees in the village, but it was only here in the city that the words 'corpse sugar' occurred to me upon smelling them. In the front gardens of the side streets death sought me out in big dahlias, which could not rein in their

163

colours in curled up clumps of blossom. For as long as I was not living under threat these city plants came to exemplify death in general. Even when I was thinking of my own death it was always a natural death, the abdication of the flesh on thick asphalt. Later, when my friends and I lived with death threats from the secret service, things changed.

When I was back on the street after agonising interrogations, my head swimming, my eyes glassy, my legs unfamiliar, as if borrowed, when I was returning home in this state the plants showed me what could not be said in words. To do so, they needed nothing more than the smells, colours and shapes they possessed and the place where they were standing. They enlarged what had happened into a monstrosity, added to the enlargement the shrinking that was needed to survive, to place what has only just occurred among the events of the past. The dahlia showed me that I should see the interrogation as the official duty of the interrogator, that the notches in the small table were from all those who were interrogated before me and would be after me, that I was one case among many, yet a single case. What really upset me was the stuff of daily life for the interrogator, nothing but routine in his hideous profession – that's what the dahlia showed me. Also that the routine practised on me becomes specific to me, that I must think through this specific treatment personally and must protect myself. I must believe myself worthy of defending, even if before and after me others have been subjected to similar treatment. How can I explain in words that the dahlia granted me an instinctive response to the conflict outside, that when you come out of an interrogation then the dahlia resembles an interrogation, or a prison cell, when someone close to you whom you don't want to lose is in prison. That in a dahlia is a child when you are pregnant and don't want to give birth under any circumstances, because you don't want to bring the child into this shitty world, but you will go to jail for having an abortion if caught.

How much should I say when I want to say everything to the girlfriend who asks me about the details of the interrogations. To say everything means: everything that can be expressed in words. So each time I told her all the facts, but nothing beyond the facts, not a word about plants that help me understand the state I'm in as I walk past the gardens on my way home. I never spoke of the peach crones, never mentioned the corpse sugar and the dahlias. Silence and speech were in balance. When silence was misunderstood by my friend I had to talk, if speech were to bring me too near the insane I had to keep silent. I didn't want to come across to her as either weird or laughable. We were close friends, we saw each other every day. But we remained different, that's what made the friendship so close. Each of us needed from the other what we didn't have ourselves. It was a closeness that didn't need to be put into words. She was not familiar with my guiding principles, she had never come across the audacity of plants. She was a child of the city. Wherever my senses stumbled I could see hers gliding, where I wavered she went forth – that's why I liked her. She would have laughed at me if

I'd spoken to her of the waxworks of the forms of death in the blooming of a valley. She didn't know the misery of being alone in the landscape, the unpaid bill of transience that cannot be withstood. She had retained a balance in everything, kept an outsider's perspective, never pondered over the right word. Instead she loved clothes and jewellery, despised the regime as the bankruptcy of all sensuality. The regime didn't come after her. She had studied welding technology, her subject was considered constructive and loyal to the state, what I did was destructive. She didn't speak a word of German and had no idea what I wrote. Perhaps for this reason the regime considered our friendship to be an unpolitical woman's matter. But it was highly political because it was so unpredictably natural. She rejected subservience out of a sense of physical disgust and was morally more uncompromising than many people with their political theories and subversive talk. I depended on that friend. When I was falling apart she was wholeness. Her behaviour was whole, but unbeknownst to both of us death was attacking her body. She had cancer, it was discovered too late. She had three years to live, and I was emigrating. She came to visit and showed me the scar where the right breast had been removed and confessed that she had been sent by the secret service – was visiting me under orders. She was to let me know I was on the death list, that I would be cleared out of the way if I continued to speak contemptuously of Ceauşescu in the West. She had betrayed me when she arrived in Berlin, and while she admitted her betrayal, she maintained that she could never do anything to harm me. And after two days I made her pack her bags and took her to the station. And on that platform I refused the handkerchief to wave goodbye, the handkerchief for my tears. I didn't need the handkerchief to put a knot in so I didn't forget – the knot was in my throat.

She died of cancer two years after this premature departure. To love someone then have to leave them, because, without knowing what she was doing, she put her feelings for me at the disposal of the secret service, and against my own life. She had loaned our friendship to the king, who bowed down before her and wanted to kill me, and believed she would get it back, as it was when I trusted her. To betray me she must have lied to herself, they went hand in hand. The loss of this friendship has cut a swathe through my life to this day. I had to find the 'heart-beast' and the 'king' for this woman. Both concepts are double-edged, they haunt the thicket of love and betrayal. While writing, I had to ask the sentences that were inadequate, 'Why and when and how does tightly tied love get mixed up with murder.'[17] Even when you leave someone because you have to you are not without feelings of guilt. To round off the chapter about my friend I had to reach for a beautiful Rumanian folk song.

He who loves and leaves
shall feel the wrath of God
God shall punish

with the pinching beetle
the howling wind
the dust of the earth

There was nothing more to be said. The song is well known in Rumania, it came to me just as maybe prayers come to others. If you don't believe in prayer, you start miming. This song to me is like the dahlias in the garden. Like them, it manages to integrate a loss into the chain of all the other damage.

I both admire and fear plants that have hairy, creeping, overly thin stalks, deeply serrated, scratchy leaves, and fruit the size of heads. Silent heads whose face of garish flesh grows inwards: pumpkins and melons. They take on weights that, left to their own devices, they cannot carry. They spread themselves wide, climb along the ground or up fences, don't support the weight of the fruit. Their bearing is fragile, they lay their heads back against a raw field, hang vertically from the wood fence. As a child in the village I understood from these plants how a sentence from the church transforms into plants. The sentence: 'Bear ye one another's burdens' (Letter of St Paul to the Galatians 6,2). These plants help you see from the outside how it would feel if something were taken away from inside you. I wanted to learn from these plants how it would work with people. But it couldn't work. My father had to bear his drunkenness alone. No one could take away my mother's crying, and if I cried along with her, I was not crying for the same reason as she was crying. She was crying because she had a drunk-ard for a husband, who brandished a knife whenever she tried to take him to task. But I was crying because I wanted to have a mother who sometimes cried for me, for a child who didn't know why it belonged to these two parents, when this father was too drunk to be a father to his child, and this mother suffered so much from his drunkenness that her child became incidental. And my grandfather had to carry around his endless receipt books alone, and my grandmother her prayer-book with the photo of her fallen son.

In this house and home, in our silence, we kept narrowly missing each other. Our goods and chattels belonged together, our heads were entirely separate. There we were, three generations in one house. If you are not in the habit of talking you are not in the habit of thinking in words. To be present you don't have to speak. That was an instinctive approach, one that dahlias rather than people had in the city. Once you get used to this approach you are unaware that you are not speaking. You don't think about speaking, you are enclosed in silence, keeping an eye on others.

As a child in the village I wasn't familiar with the question people close to you often ask: 'What are you thinking about?' Nor did I know the frequent response: 'Nothing'. The answer that is generally not accepted and seen as an excuse, a diversion. The assumption is that we all always think about something and know what it is. I believe one can think about 'nothing', that is about something, when you don't know what it is. If you don't think in words you have thought 'about nothing', you can't say what you have thought in words. You have thought something that does not require the outline of the word. It lies in your head. Speech flies off, silence lies and lies and smells. It smelled like the spot in the house where I stood, all at sea, among the others. In the yard silence smelled like acacia blossoms or freshly mown clover, in the sitting room like mothballs or a row of quinces on the cupboard, in the kitchen like dough or meat. Each of us had steps inside our head that silence walked up and down. The question: 'What are you thinking about?' would have been an assault. It was self-evident that one was full of secrets. When we spoke of work and other matters each of us talked straight past our secrets, which, because they were there, proved that we belonged together. Also that I belonged with those in the house. It was down to me rather than to them that I looked at them for too long, caused them to turn eerie, to question me. That I became such short-lived matter in the face of their substance with its natural durability was my own failing.

I mentioned the melon, for the biblical sentence: 'Bear ye one another's burdens' turned into a plant in the form of a melon. The melon demonstrates how comfortably silence as an instinctive approach can sit in your head your whole life if you feel it's absurd to waste thoughts in speech. I liked going to church on Sunday mornings, it was a chance to avoid peeling potatoes. No one else in our house went to church, so I was allowed to go, representing the others. For public opinion this was beneficial, and perhaps the people in the house also thought if the child goes to pray, God will understand that the rest of the family has no time.

My grandmother believed in God, prayed every morning and evening at home. After her son fell in the war she went only once a year to church, on Remembrance Day. And on that day I always sat beside her. I was attracted to the large plaster figure of the Virgin Mary in the church, you could see her heart. It was on the outside, painted on the full-length pale blue dress, large and dark red with a few black specks. She was pointing to her heart with her raised index finger. The heart was so badly painted it was good. Unintentionally the village painter tipped it over into something it didn't have to be. Sometimes when I'd been sent to the village in the middle of the day to do some shopping I stepped briefly into the church. It wasn't a church for me when I was there alone. I went to see Mary, didn't cross myself or curtsy. In the cool the crickets chirped behind the altar, as they did in the evenings in our yard. I went straight for Mary, took a close look at her heart, sucked on a sweet I had bought with the change and placed one for her next to her bare toes. Or a piece of thread if I had bought a cotton reel, or a match from the box, a sewing needle or a hair clasp. Then I went back to the street. Once I'd placed a drawing pin next to her toes and when I was halfway out the door I turned round and took it back, in case she stepped on it. I never prayed to her, never gave her a flower.

171

From winter through spring and into summer every time I looked at it her heart was a watermelon cut in two. Remembrance Day wasn't till autumn and my grandmother came with me to church. I whispered in her ear, 'Look, Mary's heart is half a watermelon.' Her knee jiggled, for we were surrounded by people, then she stroked my knee, as if accidentally, and whispered, 'That may be, but you mustn't talk about it.' Then she jiggled her knee a few more times, as if to show she was doing it for herself and not as a sign that I should listen carefully. On the way home she came back to the subject so briefly that in the words the silence was already present. She merged the black-flecked heart and the cut open watermelon into the brief words THAT THING. 'You must never say THAT THING about Mary to anyone.' I kept to it even after she was dead, even after I moved to the city. I had nothing to say about it until I began to write.

From the outside perhaps writing resembles talking. From the inside it's a matter of being alone. Written sentences are to lived facts what silence is to speaking. When I put lived experience into sentences a ghostly move begins. The guts of facts are packed into words, they learn to walk and move house to a place as yet unknown. To stay with the image of the house move, when I write it's as if the bed is in a forest, the chair in an apple, the street in a finger. But the opposite is also true: the handbag becomes bigger than the city, the whites of the eye bigger than the wall, the watch bigger than the moon. Places form part of the experience, an open or closed sky above one's head and the earth, asphalt or a floor under one's feet. One is surrounded by different times of day, has light or dark before one's eyes. There is a counterpoint, people or just objects. One has the beginning, the duration and the end of an event as a measure, one feels the brevity or the length of time on the skin. And none of it has anything to do with words. Lived experience doesn't give a damn about writing, is incompatible with words. Real experience can never be captured one to one by words. In order to describe it, it must be cut out to suit the words and entirely reinvented. To enlarge, diminish, simplify, complicate, include, omit – a tactic that has its own paths and that uses lived experience merely as a pretext. While writing, one drags lived experience into another field. One tests which word is capable of what. It's no longer day or night, village or city. Noun and verb are now in control, main clause and subordinate clause, beat and sound, line and rhythm. What really happened persists as a side issue, through words one gives it one shock after another. When it no longer recognises itself, it's back in the middle. To write about it one has to demolish the grandiosity of lived experience, leave that real street and turn into an invented one, for only the invented one can resemble the real one again.

And one cannot and must not allow what is precious to run aground, unprotected, to wreck it with a bad sentence. At the back of my mind when I write is always the thought that those who are precious to me will be reading it, even if they are dead, especially if they are dead. I'd like to do them justice with words. That's the only measure I know of to judge whether my sentences are good enough. While writing, this is a moral obligation, however naïve and fragmented. It was and is the opposite of standing above it, of any and all ideology – and therefore the best means of combating it. Ideology keeps an eye on everything. It decides whether sentences are allowed or forbidden. So as not to stray from what is allowed, ideologically driven authors continually plumb new variations of existing components in the text. They vary only provided the whole does not come into question. An inner moral obligation held for entirely private reasons is confusing to the lover of ideology, feels no obligation to the whole, knows that every text veers away from the predictable, flees the site offered by ideology. Sentences written out of an inner obligation consider themselves as truthful or mimed rather than allowed or forbidden.

Writing makes sentences out of lived experience, but never a conversation. The facts, as they happened, could not have endured the words later used to write them down. Writing always seems to me a tightrope walk between revealing and keeping secret. But it changes step between the two. While revealing something the real bends into the invented, and with that which is invented the real shines through, precisely because it's not formulated. Half the effect of the sentence upon reading is not formulated. This unformulated half makes the disconnection in the head possible, gives rise to the poetic shock, which we can call thinking without words. Or perhaps: feeling.

Objects are always changing according to their use, I've never worked out what many of them are. My mother pressed her largest knife into my hand and sent me up to the loft next to the chimney in the smokehouse. The hams were hung there. I was to cut off a slice and bring it to the kitchen. As I climbed the stairs I asked myself why she wasn't afraid I might do something else with the knife. I could fall and injure myself by mistake. I could cut my hand rather than the ham. I could also kill myself deliberately with the knife. If I'd done something other than cut ham with it the knife would have become something other. I stretched out time, lingered on the floor. It struck me as indifference or even neglect when, once I was back in the kitchen, my mother took the ham and the knife calmly from my hand. Nothing crossed her mind other than cutting the ham, she never asked herself why I was gone so long with the big knife.

People say 'the handkerchief', but which handkerchief. The handkerchief you cry into is not the one you wave goodbye with, not the one you use to bind a wound, not the one you use to blow your nose, and not the one you put a knot in to jog your memory, and not the one you wrap your money in so as not to lose it, and not the handkerchief that is lying on the side of the road because someone has lost it or thrown it away. The same handkerchief is never exactly the same. How many unspoken possibilities are there in this simple-sounding sentence, 'The woman puts her handkerchief in her pocket'?

One summer evening in the cemetery the neighbour's boy said to me, 'For the souls of the dead the world is no bigger than a hand-kerchief.' We were sent to the cemetery late in the evening when the heat of the day had subsided and just before it was pitch-black, the flowers on the graves should only be watered when it was cool. There was a pond behind the chapel. The croaking of the frogs reached the sky. When we swung the watering can into the pond to fill it, frogs as big as your fist flopped from the leaves on the surface into the water, a dull sound like clumps of earth on coffin lids, as if at one's own funeral one were hearing in the coffin the final greeting of the clods above one's head. We carried the full watering cans and watched a white haze rising from the graves that didn't concern us. We each watered our own flowers. It was fast work, the earth was thirsty. Then we sat together on the chapel steps and pointed out to each other the graves from which souls were flying. Not to scare off the souls we said not a word. A soul once flew out of an empty grave. Like my grandmother's son, the dead man had fallen in the war far from here, his soul a scrawny chicken. On the gravestone was written: Rest in Peace in Foreign Soil.

We didn't speak about the souls till we were on our way home. In each case we agreed upon an animal. There were lizard souls, par-tridge souls, snow goose-, hare- and crane souls. The souls of the dead fly everywhere, said the neighbour's boy, for them the world is no bigger than a handkerchief.

How can a shroud in the grass come to look in a photograph like a handkerchief. How can a photo of a son's body come to serve as a bookmark in a mother's book of prayer. How can a death fit on a sepia photograph no bigger than a matchbox. How can it make itself so small and still leave a margin of a finger's breadth for the grass. On the handkerchief in the grass my grandmother's son, ripped to shreds by a mine during the war, looks like a handful of rotten leaves blown together by the wind. How does a photo from the front have the nerve to be the announcement of a death, a shroud and a handkerchief, to confuse a human being with foliage. No one could take away the loss of her son from my grandmother. Just as the apricot trees reminded me of my dead father, an accordion reminded her of her dead son. The accordion was the object he'd left behind, to represent him. Despite the hump the accordion case resembled a coffin. Her son was so mangled when he was put in a mass grave near Mostar you could probably have fit two of him into the case. She revered this accordion coffin with its hump. It stood in the best room between the tiled stove and the bed. Your eye was drawn to it when you came through the door. Sometimes when everyone else in the house was far enough away in the garden, I opened the case and gazed at the accordion. The black and white keys looked like the white shroud and the black grass in the photo. The accordion case was my grandmother's cult object. Every day she entered the room that was inhabited not by us but by the accordion case. She looked mutely at the case, the way people look at saints in church and pray for help in silence. She had her dead son right there in the house, forgot that an accordion can never be a person, that an accordion doesn't care to whom it belongs. How does a mother come to mistake an accordion for her son. What sentences are adequate to describe how loss transforms itself into an object, which for incomprehensible reasons offers itself up as a projection of the vanished person. And how did her husband, who until 1945 owned land round the village and grain and a grocery store, then once dispossessed by socialism owned nothing but a chest full of receipt books instead of trainloads of grain or coffee beans, how did he come to note down his negligible daily shopping in the columns for ton weights. The first column is: Name of Consignment – and he writes: 'Matches'. The second column is: Quantity of Goods Trucks/Tons – and he writes: '1 Box'. The third column is: Value in Hundred Thousands/Millions – and he writes: 2 Lei/05 Bani (1 Euro and 5 cents). The land, the agricultural machinery, his bank accounts, his gold bars, socialism took all this from him. His house too and the farmyard with its outbuildings belonged to the state. He was allowed to live in just two rooms along with his wife, daughter and son-in-law. All the other rooms were used for storage: wheat and barley and corn from floor to ceiling. From early summer to late autumn the trucks drove to the rear gate laden and left the front gate empty. After socialism had concluded the dispossession of the 'exploiter class' my grandfather was so poor he could no longer afford to go to the barber. He was left with only the receipt books he had ordered in advance, which would have been enough for ten years of trading. They occupied a large chest.

In the midst of this humiliation my grandfather began to record his trivia in the columns. 'So my head doesn't get rusty,' he said. But he was seeking support in this practice, which was documenting his decline. He was looking for dignity by confronting his fall. But he never complained, just wrote down his negligible purchases from the village shop in the columns: 1 metre wick for paraffin lamp, 3 metres trouser elastic, 1 tube toothpaste, or 1 glass mustard. He calculated the day's expenditure, followed by the week, the month, the year. Perhaps the printed columns and what he entered by hand in his destitution showed him, silently, as much as the dahlias showed me in the garden after my interrogation. Or as much as the poems I recited to myself daily for courage, always poems that confirmed my life was hopeless. No one could talk my grandfather out of those damned receipt books. It wasn't till I was in the city and had got into the habit of reciting poems that I understood his receipt books were not his prayers, but his poems. Maybe even his dahlias.

Because I grew up around plants in the village I invested the city plants with certain intentions. Cedar and spruce trees in the city were as malevolent as corn in the village. They were the plants of the rulers, and dahlias and poplars were the plants of the weak. Cedar and spruce served power as living evergreen fences around government buildings and private villas. Whether you like it or not, pine cones and the seed pods of the cedar look like miniature urns. These plants had gone against their own nature, I was convinced they were loyal to the state. Gladioli also belonged among the masters' plants. As celebratory bouquets of the regime they stretched out along the rostra over delicate ferns that had long since withered. Gladioli like blooming truncheons and red carnations like party badges. There were masters' animals too: the gulls along the Danube that ate human flesh and the watchdogs of the police, prison guards and border guards. The columns of ants only ate holes in the walls of the poor, only their skin was tormented by fleas and lice. And flies. When we got together in the evening, my friends and I used to play a game with flies. It was called: 'The self-criticism of the fly'. We put the light on in the kitchen and we all sat around the table in the dark sitting room. Then one of us would stand up, turn the kitchen light off and the sitting room light on. As soon as the sitting room was lit we called out the name of a secret service man we had agreed on. Flies are drawn to the light, so after a few seconds the secret service man flew into the room as a buzzing fly. It landed first of all on the table, because the light was brightest there. We laughed hysterically, commented on the flight of the fly as it buzzed through the room. Sometimes we played the game the other way round. We gave the fly one of our names, repeated the game until we had all entered the room as flies. Until the fly had established that our number was complete, because we all still existed. At that time we all still existed, later on no longer. Then came the dark side. Perhaps

180

that's why later on, instead of playing with the fly, I played with words cut out of newspapers:

Through an apple's core
silence flies
like ladies and their dogs
like names in newspapers
investigators in the summer
hungry for wind and earth
and in the dark side of the throat
a fly
that came from the kitchen

What we so blandly call history was for each member of my family from National Socialism through the fifties the dark side of the throat. Each of them was summoned by history, had to report to history as perpetrator or victim. And when history dismissed them none was unscathed. My father deadened his time as an SS soldier with drink. My mother got into fights with half-starved shaven-headed women, deportees like herself, my grandmother revered the accordion case, my grandfather clung to his receipt books. In their heads things that should never have been there collided. I never understood the damage to my relatives until I myself succumbed to hopelessness. Only then did I know that one's nerves remain forever shattered from too violent an assault. That this strain manifests itself in later years and reaches back to an earlier time. It changes not only subsequent things, but previous ones that have nothing to do with the rift in one's life, when the rift didn't exist. Everything becomes magnetised by this gulf, nothing in one's head or in one's life can be separated from it. What happened before the rift seems in retrospect as if it was in hiding, but even then it was an announcement of the loss to come, a prologue to be ignored at your peril.

When I was seventeen, I went for the first time on a school trip to the Black Sea. The water was green with white foam. To my green, village eye it looked like the biggest, flattest meadow I had ever seen, with the most cuckoo flower that could ever grow. A meadow full to overflowing. I was familiar with the vast, green pasture land rubbing against the edge of the sky, so flat that every person could be seen from far off. This openness left one feeling exposed and visible, so transparent from toes to fingers that one was almost consumed by the sky. The head collapsed, but never the ground beneath. I probably ventured full of trust into the deep water of the grassland without thinking that I couldn't swim. The ground was gone, the brimming meadow became water, deep enough to drown in. I made no attempt to swim, thought only, now the sea will eat me. I lost consciousness and came to on the shore with a crowd of people round me. Someone had seen me drowning and dragged me on to dry land in time. I was so confused I didn't think to ask who'd saved me. I didn't even say thank you. The next day, when I finally asked, they all shrugged and said: a stranger who walked away from the crowd right after giving artificial respiration.

During the remaining eleven days of the holiday the water was off limits for me. I spent my time in cafés on the asphalt as if the sea were nowhere near, but wherever I was I had visions of drowning. Water was endlessly filling my ears. After the terror came a calmness as I was drowning, and I couldn't shake it off. Later I spoke about the sea, but said nothing to people at home about drowning. The hunger of the sea for flesh I kept to myself, just as I didn't speak about the hunger of the fields for flesh. When I didn't speak, the terror fell asleep inside me. When I did, it awoke. And when I wrote about it I moved the locale, dreamed up glacial lakes in the mountains, they were high up and closer to the sky.

Ten years after I almost drowned in the sea, I was so weary of the secret service's harassment I thought of putting an end to this shitty life by drowning myself in the river. I still couldn't swim. That was good. I still hated the malevolence of water. On the river bank I put two stones in my coat pockets. It was spring, a weak sun, the fresh poplar shoots smelled bitter-sweet like caramel. I was mildly euphoric at the thought that I could swerve away from this encirclement. Steal quietly and cunningly away from life, I thought, and the next time the interrogator wants to dismantle me I'm not available. And he stands there, monstrously alone in the patches of sunlight on the damned floor. That I would take my own life, a life I would have liked had it not been such a mess, was no longer relevant. Aside from the fear of being killed, I no longer existed for myself. Today it seems illogical, I felt the fear because I wanted to live. But my nerves were so shot, and I was so fixated on those who spread fear, that to remove myself from them felt like a triumph. The revenge against them with my planned suicide was so clear that it didn't occur to me how irreversibly I'd be taking revenge on myself.

I had forced into my coat pockets two stones so large the pocket flaps no longer closed. All was set, but why did I place the stones back on the ground. I took note of the spot on the river bank where they lay. I knew them and they knew me, and I knew we would find each other if it had to be. I was at peace with myself, and I returned calmly into the city. I'd practised death and now knew the movements needed to get hold of it. It let me move away, but it was not unfriendly. I took it as a postponement, because the water was still cold, the spring sun licked at it drowsily. Later, I wrote about it: 'Death was whistling for me from afar, I needed to sprint to get to him. I almost had myself under control, only a tiny bit of me refused to go along. Maybe it was my heart-beast.'[18]

And much later I put words cut from newspapers together as a collage, so my real river stones could shine through in invented ones:

in the middle of the day Heinrich walked out of the office
above the canal a bird sang to the wind
the sky's birthmark

it swung along the wire like a trouser seam
Heinrich walked on stones
the largest of the small in his pockets
so glittering and heavy
as if he'd never been alive
his only desire water deep enough to sink into
in the fist of an ash tree the bird has a nest
and in its face a singing engine
and nun black clothes

Like so much else, the secret service confiscated my wish to withdraw through drowning a few days after I had practised it with stones on the river bank. An interrogator I didn't know visited me in the factory, locked my office door from the inside, placed the key on the table, sat down and asked for water. As he watched I poured mineral water into a glass. Never has it taken so long to fill a glass with water. Although I myself didn't know what I was thinking at that moment, it seemed to me he could see it, running through me like a script. Although he had locked the door, the way he waited suggested he could only arrive once the glass was full. Then it was full, I hadn't spilled a drop. The water in the glass fizzed and the air seemed frozen. Such was the silence between him and me that you could hear the bubbles crackling. Then he began screaming, worked himself into a rage and forgot about his glass of mineral water. He spread his elbows so wide on the table and strained his shoulders so hard that he had to pull in his neck. It shredded his voice. The artery in his neck throbbed like blue wire. He was sitting on my chair so I stood with my back against the cupboard, chirping a meaningless phrase here and there. My fear looked like calm. He must have realised he was getting nowhere, so he changed tack. He swallowed, wiped his forehead with the back of his hand, suggested I was taking him for a fool even though I hadn't said anything of consequence, and made his voice sound calm. He raised the tip of his tie, placed it next to the glass on the table, stared at it as if he were counting the stripes, and said, as if making peace, 'Fine, we'll put you in the water.' Then he lifted the glass from the table along with the tip of the tie, which fell back on to his stomach, and emptied the glass in one slug. As he wiped his mouth I thought of my two stones by the river and knew it wouldn't happen again. 'I will never drown myself. He wants my death, he's threatening me with the river, he'll have me to deal with. Let him be so obliging as to do his dirty work himself.' From that day on I stayed well away from the river, so far away I no longer knew where the stones were, not even when I crossed the river in a tram. The sun had slid into summer, the water was no longer cold. Near my stones, verdigris grey thistles were blooming.

The secret service didn't do the dirty work for me, nor I for them. I was so disgusted by his drinking a glass of water in one slug then talking of drowning, that the minute he was gone I poured the remaining water in the bottle down the sink and threw his glass in the waste-paper basket, to make sure I never drank from it again.

The following morning it was back on my desk. The cleaning lady probably thought it had ended up in the waste-paper basket by accident. To be sure I was getting rid of it I put the glass in my handbag when work was over, and on my way home I hurled it against a concrete post in a dusty side street. A lorry was going by, I didn't hear the shattering of the glass, it was as quiet as the fizzing water the day before. Something a friend once said to me was going round and round in my head. We'd been talking about the Rumanian language, and he'd said, 'What kind of language is it that doesn't have a word for floater.' This sentence became a consolation for me after the water drinker's threats: if there's no word for floater in Rumanian, I thought, the secret service can't possibly drown me. I can't become something for which there's no word in his language. This wordless place in the Rumanian vocabulary felt like a gap. My hope was, they won't get me, if things turn nasty I'll vanish, slide in to where there is no word. I told my friends about the interrogation, described the tie, the drinking of the water. But I didn't mention emptying the bottle, throwing away the glass. And certainly not the gap through which I wanted to vanish.

Late one summer I saw the body of a young woman in the paupers' cemetery. She disabused me of the notion that one can't be drowned because there's no word for a drowned body in Rumanian. She gave me a shock, and I gave her two cherries by way of thanks.

One of my friends had had his flat ransacked again in his absence. Yet again the house search was staged as a burglary. We knew the game. It was repeated a few times every year with each of us. They rummaged through books and papers, ripped pictures from their frames, tore open the seam of the curtain. Gold and jewellery were untouched. When the search was finished a single small object of no consequence would be taken: an alarm clock, a watch, a transistor radio. And before they left they would damage the front door to give the impression of a burglary. The police were invariably there when one got home. The house search was recorded as a burglary because of the one missing object. At some point a summons to a trial would arrive. The object taken by the secret service would be foisted on some prisoner doing time for theft. The prisoner would be produced and had to admit that he was the burglar. At the time my friend was missing a small transistor radio, and he was told that the thief Ion Seracu had died in prison. My friend wanted the court to give him the address of his family – he was told there were no living relatives, the dead man had no one. We wanted to check this information. Knowing that dead people with no relatives ended up in the paupers' cemetery we went to the cemetery. Also because of the strange name that had been attached to the supposed thief: Seracu. SARAC means POOR in Rumanian. The cemetery was encircled by high concrete walls and was known to be the place where the state buried its victims. It was about midday, high summer, sizzling heat. Knee-high grasses bloomed in the cemetery, their colours swaggering and garish. Scrawny stray dogs carried body parts back and forth along dirt paths, fingers, ears, toes. We found the grave bearing the name Ion Seracu. There was a bouquet of flowers on it, not grasses but roses. They were still fresh and the day was hot, they hadn't been there long. Just before we came the dead man had had a visit. From whom?

There was a concrete hut in the middle of the cemetery. Someone had written 'blood suckers' on the wall in red oil paint. The hut had a narrow doorway, no door. On the wall inside was a wash basin, and in the middle of the room a concrete table. And on the table a dead naked woman. The legs bound by wire at the ankles, the wire also around one wrist, the binding round the hand ripped open, incisions on the other wrist. Hair, face and body were coated with thick slime. The dead woman was that thing for which there is no word in Rumanian: a floater. A manacled floater was not someone who had drowned, but someone who had been drowned. On the way to the cemetery I had foolishly bought a bag of cherries, only because we were going past the market. I was at a loss, reached into the bag and put two cherries where the eyes oozed in the dead woman's head. We left, said not a word till we reached the exit, scarcely able to bend our legs. The grasses were unbearably beautiful, they were hungry for me, I could sense. I felt they would turn rigid and not let us through the gate. Were the grasses a gift of flowers for the dead, who had no one, or a blooming hiding place for the murders of the state. Or both. Or neither one nor the other, but just a stupid need under the pressure of fear to file away what one cannot bear. My friend and I told our narrow circle about the

189

roses on the grave, the hut with the bound woman. By tacit agreement neither of us said anything about the dogs and the cherries. I alone said nothing about the grasses, as was my custom from way back.

A few years later, once we had all gathered in Germany and decided to speak about the enormity of Ceauşescu's crimes, friends said to the two of us that we would be best advised not to mention the paupers' cemetery: 'No one would believe you, you'll make fools of yourselves. At best it will make people think we're crazy and no longer believe anything we say.' So I never mentioned the paupers' cemetery when I had to provide a list of the regime's horrors. I used more harmless examples and I could tell that the warning was correct; in this country, even the harmless examples seemed exaggerated. I wondered if my head was ticking right. I recall the time of the dictatorship as a life on a thin thread that made increasingly clear what could not be spoken in words.

I've not abandoned the knowledge with which we make fools of ourselves, nor been able to ignore it in my writing. I've set my heart on getting the better of the cemetery grass, on dealing with it from its reverse side and my distance in time, making it unrecognisable through invention and cutting it down to size for the word. In *The Land of Green Plums* a casual insight drawn from the paupers' cemetery keeps recurring: 'The words in our mouths do as much damage as our feet on the grass. But so do our silences.' Or: 'The grass stands tall inside our heads. When we speak it gets mowed. Even when we don't. And then the second, and the third growth springs up at will. And even so: We are the lucky ones.'[19] Or: 'I wanted love to grow back, like the grass when it's mown down. To grow differently, if need be, like children's teeth, like hair, like fingernails. To spring up at will.'[20] And later it says in the text, 'Today the grass listens when I speak of love. It seems to me that this word isn't honest even with itself.'[21]

A mother's shaved head, a father's drunkenness, a grandmother's accordion coffin, a grandfather's receipt books, the faces of a dahlia, a friend's betrayal, the double-edged beauty of cemetery grass, these could perhaps be replaced by other instances when talking about life. But these other instances too would contain things that had made the acquaintance of the 'dark side of the throat', and to them too would apply the sentence: 'When we don't speak, we become unbearable, when we do, we make fools of ourselves.'

NOTES

1. Alexandru Vona: *The Bricked Up Windows*, Bucharest, 1993.
2. Ibid.
3. Frankfurter Allgemeine Zeitung, 18 November 2000.
4. Hanna Krall: *Hypnoza*, Warsaw, 1989.
5. Vona.
6. Ibid.
7. Ibid.
8. António Lobo Antunes: *An Explanation of the Birds*, translated by Richard Zenith.
9. Antunes, Secker & Warburg.
10. Jorge Semprún: *Autobiographie de Federico Sanchez,* Éditions du Seuil.
11. Herta Müller: *Der Fuchs war damals schon der Jäger*, Rowohlt Verlag, 1992.
12. Vona.
13. Herta Müller: *The Land of Green Plums*, translated by Michael Hofmann. German title: *Herztier*.
14. Vona.
15. Herta Müller: *The Land of Green Plums*.
16. Herta Müller: *Niederungen*, Rotbuch Verlag.

17. Herta Müller: *The Land of Green Plums.*
18. Ibid.
19. Ibid.
20. Ibid.
21. Ibid.

NOTE ON THE TEXT

'Hunger and Silk' ('*Hunger und Seide*') was first published as part of the essay collection *Hunger und Seide* by Rowohlt Verlag in 1995.

The following three essays were delivered as lectures during the Tübingen poetry lectureship in 2001. They were first published as part of the essay collection *Der König verneigt sich und tötet* by Carl Hanser Verlag in 2003 and in paperback by Fischer Taschenbuch Verlag in 2008:

'In Every Language There are Other Eyes' ('*In jeder Sprache sitzen andere Augen*')

'The King Bows Down and Kills' ('*Der König verneigt sich und tötet*')

'When We Don't Speak We Become Unbearable – When We Do We Make Fools of Ourselves' (*'Wenn wir schweigen werden wir unangenehm – wenn wir reden werden wir lächerlich'*)

'Always the Same Snow and Always the Same Uncle' (*'Immer derselbe Schnee und immer derselbe Onkel'*) was originally a speech of thanks given on receiving the Berlin Literature Prize in Berlin on 4 May 2005.

'Such a Big Body and Such a Small Engine' (*'So ein großer Körper und so ein kleiner Motor'*) was originally a speech of thanks given on receiving the Walter Hasenclever Literature Prize in Aachen on 20 June 2006.

'Cristina and Her Double' (*'Cristina und Ihre Attrape'*) was developed from an article published in *Die Zeit* on 23 July 2009 and was published as *'Cristina und Ihre Attrape: oder Was (nicht) in den Akten der Securitate steht'* by Wallstein Verlag in 2009.

All three essays were published as part of the essay collection *Immer derselbe Schnee und immer derselbe Onkel* by Carl Hanser Verlag in 2011.

ABOUT THE TRANSLATOR

Geoffrey Mulligan is a publisher and editor. He lives and works in London. His translations include *Magic Hoffmann* by Jakob Arjouni, which was longlisted for the International IMPAC Dublin Literary Award in 2000.